READINGS ON

THE TAMING
OF THE SHREW

THE TAMING
OF THE SHREW

Other Titles in the Greenhaven Press Literary Companion Series:

British Authors

Jane Austen
Joseph Conrad
Charles Dickens
J.R.R. Tolkien

British Literature

Animal Farm
Beowulf
Brave New World
The Canterbury Tales
A Christmas Carol
Frankenstein
Great Expectations
Gulliver's Travels
Hamlet
Jane Eyre
Julius Caesar
Lord of the Flies
Macbeth
The Merchant of Venice
Othello
Pride and Prejudice
Romeo and Juliet
Shakespeare: The Comedies
Shakespeare: The Histories
Shakespeare: The Sonnets
Shakespeare: The Tragedies
Silas Marner
A Tale of Two Cities
Tess of the d'Urbervilles
Wuthering Heights

THE GREENHAVEN PRESS
Literary Companion
TO BRITISH LITERATURE

THE TAMING OF THE SHREW

Laura Marvel, *Book Editor*

David L. Bender, *Publisher*
Bruno Leone, *Executive Editor*
Bonnie Szumski, *Series Editor*

Greenhaven Press, Inc., San Diego, CA

Every effort has been made to trace the owners of copyrighted material. The articles in this volume may have been edited for content, length, and/or reading level. The titles have been changed to enhance the editorial purpose. Those interested in locating the original source will find the complete citation on the first page of each article.

Library of Congress Cataloging-in-Publication Data

Readings on The taming of the shrew / book editor, Laura Marvel.
    p.   cm. — (The Greenhaven Press literary companion to British literature)
  Includes bibliographical references and index.
  ISBN 0-7377-0237-0 (lib. : alk. paper) —
ISBN 0-7377-0236-2 (pbk. : alk. paper)
  1. Shakespeare, William, 1564–1616. Taming of the shrew. I. Marvel, Laura. II. Series.
PR2832 .R43   2000
822.3'3—dc21   99-059318
                                                     CIP

Cover photo: Archive Photos

Copyright ©2000 by Greenhaven Press, Inc.
PO Box 289009
San Diego, CA 92198-9009
Printed in the U.S.A.

*"I am as peremptory as she
proud-minded:
And where two raging fires
meet together,
They do consume the thing
that feeds their fury."*

—Petruchio in act II, scene 1
of William Shakespeare's
The Taming of the Shrew

CONTENTS

Chapter 1: The Structure and Characters of *The Taming of the Shrew*

The play is composed of an introductory episode, called the Induction, a main plot focused on Petruchio's taming of the shrew, Kate, and a romantic subplot concerning Kate's sister, Bianca, and her three suitors. The Induction introduces a drunken tinker, Christopher Sly, who is conveyed while unconscious to the home of a local lord; Sly is dressed up as a gentleman, and when awakened he is entertained with a play, which presents the main taming plot and the romantic subplot.

The structure of the play can be seen as a series of plays within plays. Shakespeare starts a play about the conflict between a hostess and a drunken tinker, then the lord intervenes and stages a play in which the tinker is costumed as a gentleman, after which a troupe of players arrives to stage a play for the tinker, and the players' play involves a series of characters who play roles in order to court, marry, deceive, and liberate one another. Just as Petruchio's role-playing upsets Kate's expectations and frees her from the limited role as shrew, so Shakespeare's plays-within-plays structure upsets the audience's expectations and invites audience participation.

Characters are not always what they first appear to be in Shakespeare's plays. Christopher Sly's "wife" is really a boy; Bianca is less modest, sweet, and obedient with her tutors, and later her husband, than she pretends; perhaps, then, Kate only appears tamed and obedient in the final scene, and is in reality both shrewd and in control.

Chapter 2: Themes and Ideas Developed in *The Taming of the Shrew*

Shakespeare's satire; when Kate imitates his tone she mocks his dream of mastery and asserts her own power over her husband.

Foreword

"'Tis the good reader that
makes the good book."

Ralph Waldo Emerson

The story's bare facts are simple: The captain, an old and scarred seafarer, walks with a peg leg made of whale ivory. He relentlessly drives his crew to hunt the world's oceans for the great white whale that crippled him. After a long search, the ship encounters the whale and a fierce battle ensues. Finally the captain drives his harpoon into the whale, but the harpoon line catches the captain about the neck and drags him to his death.

A simple story, a straightforward plot—yet, since the 1851 publication of Herman Melville's *Moby-Dick*, readers and critics have found many meanings in the struggle between Captain Ahab and the whale. To some, the novel is a cautionary tale that depicts how Ahab's obsession with revenge leads to his insanity and death. Others believe that the whale represents the unknowable secrets of the universe and that Ahab is a tragic hero who dares to challenge fate by attempting to discover this knowledge. Perhaps Melville intended Ahab as a criticism of Americans' tendency to become involved in well-intentioned but irrational causes. Or did Melville model Ahab after himself, letting his fictional character express his anger at what he perceived as a cruel and distant god?

Although literary critics disagree over the meaning of *Moby-Dick*, readers do not need to choose one particular interpretation in order to gain an understanding of Melville's novel. Instead, by examining various analyses, they can gain numerous insights into the issues that lie under the surface of the basic plot. Studying the writings of literary critics can also aid readers in making their own assessments of *Moby-Dick* and other literary works and in developing analytical thinking skills.

The Greenhaven Literary Companion Series was created with these goals in mind. Designed for young adults, this unique anthology series provides an engaging and comprehensive introduction to literary analysis and criticism. The essays included in the Literary Companion Series are chosen for their accessibility to a young adult audience and are expertly edited in consideration of both the reading and comprehension levels of this audience. In addition, each essay is introduced by a concise summation that presents the contributing writer's main themes and insights. Every anthology in the Literary Companion Series contains a varied selection of critical essays that cover a wide time span and express diverse views. Wherever possible, primary sources are represented through excerpts from authors' notebooks, letters, and journals and through contemporary criticism.

Each title in the Literary Companion Series pays careful consideration to the historical context of the particular author or literary work. In-depth biographies and detailed chronologies reveal important aspects of authors' lives and emphasize the historical events and social milieu that influenced their writings. To facilitate further research, every anthology includes primary and secondary source bibliographies of articles and/or books selected for their suitability for young adults. These engaging features make the Greenhaven Literary Companion Series ideal for introducing students to literary analysis in the classroom or as a library resource for young adults researching the world's great authors and literature.

Exceptional in its focus on young adults, the Greenhaven Literary Companion Series strives to present literary criticism in a compelling and accessible format. Every title in the series is intended to spark readers' interest in leading American and world authors, to help them broaden their understanding of literature, and to encourage them to formulate their own analyses of the literary works that they read. It is the editors' hope that young adult readers will find these anthologies to be true companions in their study of literature.

INTRODUCTION

William Shakespeare's *The Taming of the Shrew* has alternately delighted and disturbed generations of spectators and readers. The battle of the sexes at the heart of this drama is one reason for the play's continuing appeal, but it is also the source of ongoing controversy about the central taming plot. Is the battle of the sexes a boisterous battle of wits or sexual warfare pressing toward brutality and misogyny? As a result of Petruchio's taming methods, is Kate liberated from the confining role of shrew? educated about social roles? awakened to love? confirmed in secret mastery of her husband? or forced into submission by a domineering husband? Such issues as the play's genre and the purpose of the introductory episode depend on one's interpretation of the battle of the sexes. Spectators and critics question the genre of the play. Is it a farce? a romantic comedy? a satire? a problem play? Directors and readers contemplate the introductory episode. Why does the play begin with two scenes about a drunken tinker, Christopher Sly? Why does Sly disappear from the play after act 1?

Over the centuries numerous adaptations and offshoots inspired by *The Taming of the Shrew* have attempted to resolve the problematic taming and submission of Kate and the seemingly unfinished Christopher Sly plot. David Garrick's eighteenth-century adaptation, *Catherine and Petruchio*, eliminated both the introductory episode and the subplot in order to focus on a brutalized and intensified battle between the warring lovers. Benjamin Webster's nineteenth-century version highlighted the introductory episode by costuming the Lord and Sly as Shakespeare and fellow actor Richard Tarlton. Twentieth-century productions have been equally diverse: Charles Marowitz's 1975 adaptation, *The Shrew*, interpreted the taming of Kate as brutal brainwashing. In Wilford Leach's popular 1978 production, Raul Julia and Meryl Streep emphasized role-playing in their approach to the courtship. Cole Porter's 1948 musical, *Kiss Me Kate*, re-created the entire play as "a story of actors whose tempestu-ous love life offstage reflects the difficulties of the wooers they portray."[1] This uniquely unsettling play provokes re-sponse and invites debate.

The Taming of the Shrew is one of Shakespeare's most timely plays, since the battle of the sexes rages as strongly today as it did in 1594; it also remains a play subject to mul-tiple, mutually exclusive interpretations. Part of Shake-speare's genius is to capture in a play subjects of enduring human interest and present them in such a way that each actor, director, reader, and critic is compelled to bring to the play what he or she knows about human interaction in order to arrive at a meaningful interpretation. *The Taming of the Shrew* challenges each of us to read, react, question, and de-bate. Attentiveness to the text of the play and willingness to consider multiple interpretive possibilities allow each of us to enjoy this provocative play while clarifying our own sense of the relationship between self and society, men and women.

The essays selected for the Greenhaven Literary Compan-ion to Shakespeare's *The Taming of the Shrew* provide teach-ers and students with a wide range of information and opin-ion about the play and its author's style, themes, and outlook on the human condition. All of the authors of the essays are, or were (until their deaths), noted English-language experts, professors at leading colleges and universities, and/or schol-ars specializing in Shakespearean studies. Each of the es-says in this literary companion explains or discusses in de-tail a specific, narrowly focused topic. The introduction to each essay previews the main points, and inserts inter-spersed within the essays exemplify ideas expressed by the authors, offer supplementary information, and add authen-ticity and color. Inserts are drawn from *The Taming of the Shrew* or other plays by Shakespeare, from critical commen-tary about these works, and from other scholarly sources.

Above all, this companion book is designed to enhance the reader's understanding and enjoyment of the controver-sial early comedy, *The Taming of the Shrew*. As scholar Brian Morris states:

> The complex, dynamic, developing relationship between
> Katherina and Petruchio . . . lies at the heart of the play's ap-
> peal to the audience. It is a special example of the theme of
> "the battle of the sexes" . . . and every live performance of *The*

Shrew sets up a tension between one half of the audience and the other, a tension which can be resolved in many subtly different ways depending on the actors, the theater, the aims of the production. . . . [The play] is a marvellous exhibition of adroit dramatic balance, offering solutions while preserving uncertainties and mysteries.[2]

1. David Bevington, ed., *The Taming of the Shrew.* New York: Bantam, 1980, p. xxvii.

2. Brian Morris, ed., *The Taming of the Shrew.* London: Methuen, 1981, p. 104.

SHAKESPEARE AND *THE SHREW:* A BIOGRAPHICAL ESSAY

The Taming of the Shrew is one of Shakespeare's earliest and most controversial comedies. While many know that the main plot of the comedy focuses on the battle of the sexes courtship and marriage of Kate and Petruchio, few know how the play actually begins. *The Taming of the Shrew* is the only play by Shakespeare which opens with an "induction," a dramatic episode which introduces and frames the main action of the play. Significantly, this "induction" is set in Shakespeare's native Warwickshire and includes several references to people and places in the Stratford area. For instance, the drunken tinker, Christopher Sly, mentions "Marion Hacket, the fat alewife of Wincot" as well as one Stephen Sly. Wincot is a small village about four miles from Stratford and the parish register shows that there were Hackets living in Wincot in the late sixteenth century; moreover, an actual Stephen Sly really did live in Stratford during Shakespeare's day. Stratford, at the time of Shakespeare's birth, was a simple market town of about two thousand people in the center of a rich farming area. "Its population consisted largely of farmers, the artisans and craftsmen who served them, and the businessmen who ran stores and inns, retailed manufactured goods, and marketed the farmers' crops. . . . Stratford's principal industry in Shakespeare's day (and until this century) was the brewing of beer and ale."[1]

SHAKESPEARE OF STRATFORD

Fewer uncertainties and mysteries surround the man who created *The Taming of the Shrew*, and who set the induction of the play in Warwickshire, than is often supposed. Although Francis Bacon, Christopher Marlowe, Queen Elizabeth, and Edward de Vere, seventeenth earl of Oxford, among others, have each been nominated as the author of Shakespeare's plays, no records before the eighteenth century exist that even express doubt about Shakespeare's authorship; on the other hand, more than one hundred official documents and about fifty contemporary allusions to Shakespeare and his works do exist, which offer enough information to outline the central events of his life.

The official records document William Shakespeare's baptism at Holy Trinity Church, Stratford, Warwickshire, on April 26, 1564, and his burial fifty-two years later in the same church on April 25, 1616. Since the memorial monument records the day of Shakespeare's death as April 23, and since infants were commonly christened three days after birth, William Shakespeare's birth and death are traditionally celebrated on April 23. This date holds particular significance in England as St. George's Day, a feast day honoring the patron saint of England.

William Shakespeare was the third of eight children born to John and Mary Arden Shakespeare. At the time of William's birth, John was a glover and Mary, the daughter of a gentleman farmer, possessed a considerable inheritance. The year after William's birth, John was elected alderman and several years later bailiff (mayor) of Stratford.

Although the Stratford Grammar School attendance records no longer exist, there is no reason to doubt that Shakespeare attended school. John Shakespeare's status as an alderman of Stratford entitled his children to free education at the excellent local grammar school. Oxford-educated Thomas Jenkins was Stratford schoolmaster from 1575 to 1579 and would have taught the boys the standard curriculum: Latin grammar and literature in Latin, including the works of Ovid, Virgil, Plautus, Terence, and Seneca.

While Shakespeare probably finished his formal schooling at the usual age, fifteen or sixteen, he must have pursued his education actively and independently throughout his lifetime. His works reveal familiarity with Latin and French language and literature, ancient history (notably Plutarch), English history (primarily from Rafael Holinshed's *Chronicles*), Italian literature, and English literature from Chaucer to his contemporaries. The plays also reveal Shakespeare's considerable practical knowledge about English courtly life, the trades, the army, and the church. As scholar Harry Levin explains, Shakespeare's "frame of reference is so far-ranging, and he is so concretely versed in the tricks of so many trades, that lawyers have written to prove he was trained in the law, sailors about his expert seamanship, naturalists upon his botanizing, and so on through the professions."[2]

At the age of eighteen, Shakespeare was married to Anne Hathaway, eight years older than he. On November 27, 1582, a marriage license was issued for the couple and in May 1583 their daughter Susanna was born. Two years later twins, Hamnet and Judith, completed the Shakespeare family. No records exist to document Shakespeare's life between the birth of the twins in 1585 and the snarling reference of playwright Robert Greene to Shakespeare as the upstart actor and playwright in London in 1592, but scholars have speculated at length about Shakespeare's probable reasons for pursuing a career as an actor and playwright.

Perhaps the performances of traveling troupes of actors inspired Shakespeare's interest in theater when he was still a child. Stratford records indicate performances by two traveling theatrical troupes, the Queen's Men and the Earl of Worcester's Men, as early as 1568 when Shakespeare was a boy of five. Theatrical troupes continued to make periodic visits to Stratford during Shakespeare's boyhood and adolescence, and in 1586 the Earl of Leicester's Men played in Stratford. "[T]his fact has prompted speculation that the young Shakespeare joined them at this time and returned with them to London to begin his career, although no evidence supports this proposition."[3] Perhaps, as scholar Francois Laroque suggests, Shakespeare actually joined the Queen's Men after it had lost one of its players, William Knell, in a brawl with a fellow actor while the troupe was performing in Stratford in June 1587. "The young Shakespeare could easily have stepped in to his shoes, as experience was not required. Actors learned on the job."[4] Since there is no evidence that traveling troupes actually recruited when on the road, these speculations cannot be proven; it may well be that Shakespeare's fascination with traveling productions and the need for money to support his growing family inspired him to go to London on his own to try his luck in the theater.

SHAKESPEARE'S LONDON YEARS

Whether Shakespeare joined a theatrical troupe, then made his way to London, or whether he went to London to make money to support his growing family, as a man of the theater, Shakespeare was splendidly successful. By 1592 he had already written the three parts of *Henry VI* and was popular enough to provoke at least one rival playwright's venom. Robert Greene, a Cambridge-educated playwright, scorns Shakespeare's lack of a university education and his quick popularity when he attacks Shakespeare in his pamphlet, *Groatsworth of Wit.*

"There is an upstart crow, beautified with our feathers, that with his *tiger's heart wrapped in a player's hide* supposes he is as well able to bombast out a blank verse as the best of you, and being an absolute Johannes-factotum [jack-of-all-trades] is in his own conceit the only Shake-scene in a country."[5] The italicized phrase, which parodies a line from Shakespeare's *Henry VI, part III*: "O, tiger's heart wrapped in a woman's hide," and the reference to the "only Shake-scene" identify Shakespeare as the subject of the attack.

Between 1592 and 1594 the plague spread through London so the Lord Mayor closed the theaters in the interest of public health. During this period Shakespeare concentrated on writing poetry; his two long poems, *Venus and Adonis* and *The Rape of Lucrece,* were composed and printed. These are the only works whose publication were probably supervised by Shakespeare himself. Shakespeare does not appear to have been interested in preserving an authoritative text of any of the plays for future readers. As a practical man of the theater, he was perhaps more interested in the performance and the box-office than in preserving his works for posterity. In addition, as editor G. Blakemore Evans explains, "once a dramatist had completed a play and sold it to an acting company, he ceased to have any personal rights in it, the play becoming the property of the company, which thus controlled the uses to which the play could be put, including its publication."[6]

By 1594, when the theaters reopened, Shakespeare was a charter member of a theatrical company called the Chamberlain's Men, which in 1603 became the royal company, called the King's Men. As a permanent member of the company, Shakespeare worked with the great English actors of the time: Richard Burbage (renowned for his performances as tragic hero), Henry Condell, John Heminge, Will Kemp (famous for his comic roles), and William Sly, who probably played Christopher Sly in *The Taming of the Shrew.* Shakespeare himself is listed as an actor in the company when it performed two comedies for Queen Elizabeth in the Christmas season of 1594, and he was named a chief actor in Ben Jonson's play *Every Man in His Humour,* which was performed by the Chamberlain's company in 1598. Beginning in 1599, this company acted at the Globe Theater.

THE GLOBE THEATER

From contemporary evidence we can surmise that the Globe accommodated two to three thousand spectators. Scholar David Bevington explains the particulars of the public theaters:

> The public playhouses were essentially round, or polygonal, and open to the sky, forming an acting arena approximately 70 feet in diameter; they did not have a large curtain with which to open and close a scene, such as we see today in opera and some traditional theater. A platform measuring approximately 43 feet across and 27 feet deep . . . projected into the yard. . . . The roof . . . above the stage and supported by two pillars, could contain machinery for ascents and descents. . . . Above this roof was a hut. . . . The underside of the stage roof, called the heavens, was usually richly decorated with symbolic figures of the sun, the moon, and the constellations. The platform stage stood at a height of 5½ feet or so above the yard, providing room under the stage for otherworldly effects. A trapdoor . . . gave access to the space below. The structure at the back of the platform . . . known as the tiring-house because it was the actor's attiring (dressing) space, featured at least two doors. . . . Some theaters seem to have also had a discovery space, or curtained recessed alcove, perhaps between the two doors. . . . [A] gallery above the doors . . . extends across the back and evidently contains spectators. On occasions when the action "above" demanded the use of this space, as when Juliet appears at her "window," the gallery seems to have been used by the actors.[7]

Shakespeare held a one-eighth interest in the Globe Theater. No other Elizabethan dramatist is known to have shared in the ownership of a theater and therefore been entitled to a share of the profits. "From his acting, his play writing, and his share in the playhouse, Shakespeare seems to have made considerable money,"[8] but it is for the plays themselves that Shakespeare, in rival playwright Ben Jonson's words, reveals himself as the "Soul of the Age."[9]

STRATFORD TIES REMAIN STRONG

During his residence in London, from about 1590 to 1610, Shakespeare's association with Stratford remained strong. In 1596 his father applied for and was awarded a coat of arms, which officially made him a gentleman, and which was presumably paid for with William's earnings. Also in 1596, Shakespeare's only son and heir, Hamnet, died at the age of eleven. In the years that followed successes outstripped sorrows. In 1597 Shakespeare bought the Stratford mansion New Place for his family, and in 1598 he is recorded as a leading owner of grain in the town. Numerous records attest to Shakespeare's family and financial ties to Stratford at this time: In 1601, when his father died, Shakespeare inherited his parent's home. In 1602 and 1605 he made further investments in Stratford and bought additional property. The marriage of his daughter Susanna to Dr. John Hall in 1607, and the birth of their daughter (Shakespeare's first grandchild) Elizabeth in 1608, strengthened his ties to Stratford. Because of various entries in local records and diaries, many scholars believe that Shakespeare spent much more of his time in Stratford between 1608 and 1612. His increasing involvement in Stratford community affairs and the diminishing number of plays attributed to him during this period lend some support to this belief. By 1613 Shakespeare appears to have retired completely to Stratford. He purchased a house in Blackfriars, London, in 1613, but there is no indication that he ever lived there.

Two Decades of Plays

In the first decade of his phenomenal playwriting career, 1590 to 1600, Shakespeare concentrated on history plays and comedies. His two tetralogies of English history plays were enormously popular. The first group of four history plays, *Henry VI, parts 1, 2, and 3*, and *Richard III*, focuses on the Wars of the Roses, the thirty-year dynastic struggle (1455–1485) between two branches of the Plantagenet family for the English throne.

The second group of four history plays which Shakespeare wrote, *Richard II, Henry IV, parts 1 and 2*, and *Henry V*, focuses on the period of English history just prior to the Wars of the Roses. A much more mature sequence of plays, this second tetralogy explores the genesis of the Wars of the Roses. Shakespeare, following his source of history, *Holinshed's Chronicles*, identified the deposing of King Richard II by his cousin, the Lancastrian Henry IV, as the event which precipitated the ensuing struggle. Henry IV's reign, marked by political rebellions and troubled by the antics of his son, the rebellious Prince Hal, forms the subject of the two Henry

IV plays. While Prince Hal enjoys playing thief with his tavern companions, especially the fat knight Falstaff whose lies, laziness, and agile wit are strong temptations, Hal determines to assume his responsibilities as heir apparent by the close of *Henry IV, part 1.* Upon his father's death, Prince Hal is crowned King Henry V, and in the play that bears his name, he successfully unites the warring factions in England, renews the Hundred Years' War against France, and defeats the powerful French army against impossible odds at the battle of Agincourt. Although the English triumph over France is short-lived, and the Wars of the Roses will tear England apart when Henry V's son, Henry VI, takes the throne, the last play in the second tetralogy celebrates Henry V's military success, patriotic rhetoric, and personal charm. When he courts Katherine, the King of France's daughter, Henry V shows himself a witty lover worthy of a place in the comedies of the period.

The comedies of the 1590s, including *The Taming of the Shrew, A Midsummer Night's Dream,* and *The Merchant of Venice,* as well as *Much Ado About Nothing, As You Like It,* and *Twelfth Night,* all share a focus on the forms and fun of love. In addition, they reveal Shakespeare's interest in money, upward mobility, roles, and role-playing. The witty heroines of these comedies match and at times out-match their male counterparts.

> Several critical terms have been used to suggest the special quality of Shakespeare's comedies during this period of the later 1590s. "Romantic comedy" implies first of all a story in which the main action is about love, but it can also imply elements of the improbable and miraculous. . . . "Philosophical comedy" emphasizes the moral and sometimes Christian idealism underlying many of these comedies of the 1590s: the quest for deep and honest understanding between men and women in *Much Ado About Nothing,* the awareness of an eternal and spiritual dimension to love in *The Merchant of Venice,* and the theme of love as a mysterious force able to regenerate a corrupted social world from which it has been banished in *As You Like It.* "Love-game comedy" pays particular attention to the witty battle of the sexes that we find in several of these plays.[10]

The Taming of the Shrew clearly falls in this final category.

In the second decade of his playwriting career, 1600 to 1611, Shakespeare concentrated on tragedies, among them *Hamlet, Othello, King Lear,* and *Macbeth,* and the late romances, including *The Winter's Tale* and *The Tempest.* Shakespeare's tragedies of the period are richly charged with exploration of the depths of melancholy as well as the possibilities of individual achievement. Order and the threat of disorder, the validity of the Christian faith, and the problem and nature of evil are also thematically central. Popular scholar Norrie Epstein clarifies the dimensions of Shakespearean tragedy:

> Shakespearen tragedy exposes those dark impulses that lie below life's smooth surface: the well-regulated Danish court in *Hamlet* hides something rotten; the charming and loyal Iago [in *Othello*] is a psychopath. . . . The heroes of Shakespeare's tragedies are pushed to the limits of human endurance: a young prince is compelled to avenge the murder of his father; an exiled king wanders homeless on a stormy heath; a husband strangles his wife on their marriage bed; a loyal subject murders his king. . . . Shakespeare's greatest tragic figures are fierce absolutists who find compromise impossible. . . . Macbeth sees the creature he has become but he cannot change. Lear divides his kingdom; Hamlet swears vengeance; Othello believes Iago's lies—their fates are sealed.[11]

Shakespeare's mature tragedies reveal both soul-searching exploration and doubt; the romances, on the other hand, intimate the possibility of harmonious reconciliation following years of suffering and learning. In *The Winter's Tale* Leontes, the jealous husband, mourns sixteen years before the wife he thought dead and his daughter are returned to him. In *The Tempest* Prospero, whose brother has usurped his dukedom, spends twelve years on an unnamed island before "by accident most strange" his enemies are brought to the island, tested, taught, and reconciled. While Prospero's "our revels now are ended" speech is often read as Shakespeare's own farewell to the stage, the speech is perhaps equally important as an evocation of Shakespeare's vision of theater—its importance and its limitations. The art of the dramatist creates illusions as insubstantial as dreams, yet as potentially transforming as a journey into a new world. In Michael Bogdanov's 1978 production of *The Taming of the Shrew*, Christopher Sly falls asleep on stage and dreams himself out of Warwickshire poverty and into the role of Petruchio, who hopes to marry and thrive in Padua. Shakespeare, already married, certainly thrived both financially and professionally as a result of his journey from Stratford to the new world of theater in London. Were it not for the concern of his fellow actors, though, the text of *The Taming of the Shrew* (and seventeen other plays) would have been lost, would have been in fact as ephemeral as a dream.

On March 25, 1616, Shakespeare revised and signed his last will and testament. "This will disposes of all the property of which Shakespeare is known to have died possessing, the greater share of it going to his daughter Susanna. His recently married daughter Judith received a dowry, a provision for any children that might be born of her marriage, and other gifts. Ten pounds went to the poor of Stratford; Shakespeare's sword went to Mr. Thomas Combe; twenty-six shillings and eight pence apiece went to Shakespeare's fellow actors Hemings, Burbage, and Condell to buy them mourning rings; and other small bequests went to various other friends and relatives. An interlineation contains the bequest of Shakespeare's 'second best bed with the furniture,' that is, the hangings, to his wife."[12] Although Shakespeare's small bequest to his wife has led to much provocative conjecture concerning their marriage, Shakespeare certainly did not leave his wife destitute. By law a third of Shakespeare's estate would go to his surviving wife, so there was no need to mention this in the will.

Shakespeare died about a month after revising his will, on April 23, 1616. By 1623, seven years after his death, two substantial monuments to his memory had been established: An elaborate limestone bust, designed by stonemason Gheerart Janssen, and presumably commissioned by Shakespeare's family, was erected in Holy Trinity Church, Stratford, sometime between 1616 and 1622. Since Janssen, a Dutch stone carver, had established his business near the Globe Theater, some scholars think he may actually have known Shakespeare, and they therefore believe that the bust provides a satisfactory likeness of the man. In 1623 a second monument to Shakespeare's memory was established when Shakespeare's fellow actors, Henry Condell and John Hemings, published the First Folio. It is the earliest published collection of Shakespeare's thirty-six plays and contains eighteen plays which had not been previously printed in separate quarto editions. The First Folio is a priceless tribute to the professional achievements of Shakespeare as a playwright.

THE TEXT OF *THE TAMING OF THE SHREW*

Eighteen of Shakespeare's plays were published in his lifetime as individual books, called quartos because they were constructed of sheets of paper folded in half twice, yielding four leaves or eight pages. The first collected edition of the plays, called the First Folio, was not published until seven years after Shakespeare's death. Thirty-six plays are included in the First Folio, edited by Shakespeare's fellow actors John Heminge and Henry Condell. *The Taming of the Shrew* is one of the eighteen that first appeared in the 1623 First Folio.

The evidence accumulated by textual critics suggests that the copy text used for the Folio edition of *The Taming of the Shrew* was either Shakespeare's manuscript of the play (called Foul Papers) or a transcript of the manuscript made by a scribe for the acting company (called Fair Papers). This makes the Folio text an unusually reliable version of Shakespeare's play. The date of the play is the problem. Because "A Pleasant Conceited Historie called the taming of a Shrew" was entered on the Stationers' Register (the English guild of booksellers, publishers, and printers) on May 2, 1594, the date commonly given for the play is 1594. However, this "Historie of a Shrew" is not the same play as the Folio *The Taming of the Shrew*. It is now thought that this anonymous 1594 play was compiled from the recollections of the actors who had played Sly and Grumio in Shakespeare's *The Shrew* because they needed a text for touring the provinces during the plague years when the London theaters were closed. "A Shrew" bears many similarities to *The Shrew*, but the garbled passages, the echoes of Marlowe's *Tamburlaine* and *Doctor Faustus*, the extension of Christopher Sly's role, the changed subplot, and the generally inferior quality of the drama convince most scholars that "A Shrew" is an imperfect actors' recollection of Shakespeare's play. Many textual scholars therefore argue that the date for Shakespeare's play must be before the plague and may be as early as 1589. "A Shrew" is chiefly important as the source of speculation about whether Shakespeare originally intended a larger role for Sly. Did the actors include an epilogue in which Sly determines to tame his own wife because Shakespeare had written one and they remembered performing it? Did Shakespeare later delete additional Sly scenes for artistic purposes? Or did the actors themselves create an extended role for Sly, which Shakespeare had no part in? Although at one time "A Shrew" was considered a source for Shakespeare's play, it is now generally agreed to be a "bad quarto," an actor's imperfect recollection of the actual play.

SOURCES FOR *THE TAMING OF THE SHREW*

Scholars agree that Shakespeare's play has three plots, each with its own source or sources. The romantic subplot is derived from George Gascoigne's play *Supposes*, performed in 1566 and published in 1573 and 1587. This play is itself a translation of Ariosto's Italian drama, *I Suppositi* (1509), which is based on two Roman plays, Terence's *Eunuchus* and Plautus's *Captivi*. In Gascoigne's *Supposes*, the servant Dulippo disguises himself as the master Erostrato in order to vie with old Dr. Cleander for the hand of Polynesta. Erostrato disguises himself as a servant to woo Polynesta privately. Unlike Lucentio, his counterpart in *The Shrew*, Erostrato becomes Polynesta's lover, makes her pregnant, and is tossed into a dungeon before the complications are unraveled and the happy ending is achieved. Basically Shakespeare adapts this racy, cosmopolitan comedy to suit the standards of the English public theater.

The wife-taming plot reflects a comic misogynistic folklore tradition. Numerous folktales and songs about husbands disciplining troublesome wives exist in many cultures. One ballad, "A Merry Jest of a Shrewd and Curst Wife Lapped in Morel's Skin," printed in 1550, is often listed as a probable source since the shrewish wife has a gentle younger sister, the shrew's husband is warned by the father about the woman he proposes to marry, and the success of the husband's taming is made evident publicly at a celebratory dinner. However, the husband's taming method in the ballad differs markedly from Petruchio's method in Shakespeare's play. In the ballad, the husband beats his wife until she faints, then wraps her in the salted skin of the old plowhorse Morel to tame her. Jan Harold Brunvand examined over four hundred versions of the shrew-taming folktales to argue that Shakespeare must have known the tale developed in the oral tradition rather than derived it from any one ballad. Four elements of the oral tradition characterize Shakespeare's play as well: "the victorious youngest daughter, the taming of the shrew, the bride test for obedience, and the wager on the most obedient wife."[15] Nevertheless, Petruchio's particular method of taming Kate appears to be Shakespeare's original contribution to the tradition.

The Induction's tale of a beggar placed in a wealthy man's world, or dreaming of such a place, is equally familiar in folktale tradition. It is the subject of a number of sixteenth-century English ballads, and "The Sleeper Awakened" motif occurs in *The Arabian Nights* as well. The details in the Christopher Sly Induction, however, point to Shakespeare's creative use of a familiar tale rather than direct derivation from one source.

PERFORMANCE HISTORY

Shakespeare's play was popular enough in his lifetime to provoke a sequel by John Fletcher in 1611, *The Tamer Tamed*, in which Petruchio's second wife treats him as he had treated Kate, but after a 1633 revival and one in 1663, no performance of Shakespeare's play was recorded for nearly two hundred years. Instead a series of adaptations and spin-offs consistently held the stage until 1844 when Benjamin Webster revived the original. Such adaptations as *Sauny the Scot* (1667) and *A Cure for a Scold* (1735) emphasized the misogynistic and brutal elements of sexual warfare. David Garrick's *Catherine and Petruchio* (1754) held the stage for a century and follows this misogynistic emphasis, eliminating both the Sly Induction and the Bianca subplot to emphasize the warfare. Webster's revival of the original play marked a turning point in performance history, and Augustin Daly's 1887 production was the first in the United States.

In the twentieth century the play has reemerged as a popular favorite, not only on the stage but also in film and television versions. Jonathan Miller's BBC/Time-Life version, made for television in 1980, dispensed with the Induction and portrayed the events as a serious meditation on family life. John Cleese portrayed Petruchio as an eccentric, pragmatic social worker and Kate was portrayed as a problem child. "In Miller's view the play is expressive of a peculiarly Renaissance vision of the harmonious marriage within the orderly society: 'its spirit derives from Elizabethan Puritanism's view of the household as an orderly place in which marriage is consecrated not in the church but in the orderly procedures of domesticity.'"[14] This version is in marked contrast to the 1966 Franco Zeffirelli film, which replaced the Sly Induction with an Italian carnival world full of racing and chasing, as well as verbal and visual fights. Richard Burton's Petruchio and Elizabeth Taylor's Kate remind audiences of the actual Burton/Taylor marriage: "rowing and fighting, divorcing and remarrying, but always in love."[15]

SHAKESPEARE AND *THE SHREW*

As a very early play written by the young William Shake-speare shortly after moving from Stratford to London, *The Taming of the Shrew* is almost emblematic. The movement of the play from Christopher Sly's evocation of Warwickshire in the Induction to the play world of Kate and Petruchio's Padua intimates Shakespeare's own position early in his London years: He is tied to the people and places of home (the Slys were indeed familiar in Stratford), yet actively involved in a new world of theater, a world based on money and upward mobility, as well as on roles and role-playing, creative transformation of self and of sources. Like Petruchio, Shakespeare himself may have left for London to fill the family coffers only to discover in the process a mistress as challenging and enthralling as Kate: the theater.

As an early comedy in the canon, *The Taming of the Shrew* reveals Shakespeare's interest in themes and devices that continue to preoccupy him throughout his playwriting career. Self-conscious commentary on plays and play-acting within the plays permeates the Shakespeare canon, most obviously in *A Midsummer Night's Dream, Hamlet,* and *The Tempest,* which include inner staged plays as well. The relationship between plays, dreams, and the world is also a recurring concern, from Jacques's famous speech in *As You Like It,* "All the world's a stage," to Prospero's equally famous comment on the subject in his "our revels now are ended" speech in *The Tempest.* The idea of using a play to refract and mirror contemporary concerns is given its most explicit comment in Hamlet's advice to the players, but is prevalent in many implicit ways throughout the plays.

The degree to which this particular play has engaged contemporary interest and spawned multiple interpretations reveals the continuing importance of issues such as gender identity, male/female interaction, and the relationship between the individual and society. As scholar Robert G. Blake remarks, "*The Taming of the Shrew* remains a perennially popular stage production because its subject matter—the eternal issues surrounding relationships between men and women, and a strikingly 'modern' concern with women's identities and roles—can be performed and interpreted in various ways depending on the inclinations of the play's directors."[16]

NOTES

1. Charles Boyce, *Shakespeare A to Z: The Essential Reference to His Plays, His Poems, His Life and Times, and More.* New York: Facts On File, 1990, p. 616.

2. Harry Levin, Introduction to *The Riverside Shakespeare*, 2nd ed. Boston: Houghton and Mifflin, 1997, p. 3.

3. Boyce, *Shakespeare A to Z*, p. 365.

4. Francois Laroque, *The Age of Shakespeare.* New York: Harry N. Abrams, 1993, p. 39.

5. Sylvan Barnet, "Shakespeare: An Overview" in *The Taming of the Shrew.* New York: Signet, 1986, p. ix. Barnet quotes Robert Greene's pamphlet.

6. G. Blakemore Evans, "Shakespeare's Text," in *The Riverside Shakespeare*, p. 56.

7. David Bevington, ed., *The Taming of the Shrew.* New York: Bantam Books, 1998, p. xxxiv.

8. Barnet, *The Taming of the Shrew*, p. xi.

9. Ben Jonson, "To the Memory of My Beloved, the author Mr. William Shakespeare," prefixed to the Shakespeare First Folio of 1623.

10. David Bevington, General Introduction to *The Complete Works of Shakespeare*, 4th ed. New York: HarperCollins, 1992, p. lxvii.

11. Norrie Epstein, *The Friendly Shakespeare.* New York: Viking, 1993, p. 304.

12. Bevington, *The Complete Works of Shakespeare*, p. lxxvi.

13. Brian Morris, ed., *The Taming of the Shrew.* London and New York: Methuen & Co., 1981, p. 72. Morris explains that Jan Harold Brunvand bases his work on *The Types of the Folktale: A Classification and Bibliography* by Antti Aarne, translated and enlarged by Stith Thompson, second revision, Helsinki, 1964.

14. Graham Holderness, *The Taming of the Shrew* [Shakespeare in Performance]. Manchester and New York: Manchester University Press, 1989, p. 112. Holderness is quoting Miller, whose words were recorded in *The Shakespeare Myth*, Holderness, ed., p. 201.

15. Holderness, *The Taming of the Shrew*, p. 69.

16. Robert G. Blake, "Critical Evaluation," in *A Reader's Guide to Shakespeare* by Joseph Rosenblum. New York: Barnes & Noble Books, 1999, p. 268.

CHARACTERS AND PLOT

CENTRAL CHARACTERS IN THE INDUCTION, SET IN WARWICKSHIRE, ENGLAND

Christopher Sly. The drunken tinker who is discovered by the local lord. Sly is taken to the lord's house and dressed as a gentleman. When he awakens, Sly is convinced that he has been insane and only believed himself a tinker; he watches the play *The Taming of the Shrew* with his "wife."

The lord. The man who discovers Sly asleep on the ground and decides to play a practical joke on him: dressing him as a gentleman, ordering his page to dress as his wife, arranging a play for his evening's entertainment.

Barthol'mew, the page. The lord's page, who is ordered to dress as a woman and pose as Sly's wife.

The players. A traveling troupe that appears at the lord's house and performs *The Taming of the Shrew* for Sly and his "wife" at the lord's request.

CENTRAL CHARACTERS IN *THE TAMING OF THE SHREW*, SET IN PADUA, ITALY

Lucentio. Son of Vincentio, from Pisa, who has come to Padua to study at the university, but quickly falls in love with Bianca, disguises himself as Cambio the poetry tutor to woo her, and marries her secretly.

Tranio. Lucentio's servant, who agrees to pretend he is Lucentio in order to arrange the marriage of Lucentio and Bianca with Bianca's father, Baptista; he not only wins Baptista's consent but also cons a pedant into pretending to be Lucentio's father, Vincentio.

Biondello. The boy who serves Lucentio and Tranio when the latter is posing as Lucentio.

Gremio. The old man who is a suitor for Bianca's hand, but is outbid by the wise servant, Tranio, pretending to be Lucentio.

Hortensio. A young suitor for Bianca's hand who disguises himself as Litio, the music tutor. He later marries the Widow. He is also a friend of Petruchio.

Baptista. The father of Kate and Bianca, with whom both Tranio, dressed as Lucentio, and Petruchio must negotiate to gain consent to marry Bianca and Kate.

Bianca. The younger daughter of Baptista, the younger sister of Kate; Lucentio's beloved, who is also sought by Hortensio and Gremio.

Kate. The elder daughter of Baptista, the older sister of Bianca; the shrew of the title, who marries Petruchio.

Petruchio. Hortensio's friend from Verona who desires a rich wife, courts Kate, and marries her.

Grumio. Petruchio's witty servant; not to be confused with Gremio, the old man who wishes to wed Bianca.

Vincentio. Lucentio's father, whom Kate and Petruchio meet as they journey to Padua to celebrate Bianca's wedding.

The Pedant. A man from Mantua whom Tranio tricks into pretending to be Vincentio in order to verify the claim to wealth he has made in his bid for Bianca.

The Widow. A rich woman whom Hortensio marries when he believes Bianca is changeable in her affections. Based on the final scene in the play, she appears to wear the pants in their relationship.

THE PLOT

The Taming of the Shrew is a five-act play preceded by a two-scene Induction. The Induction is an introductory episode that serves as a prologue to the work that follows. Christopher Sly, a drunken tinker, is discovered by the local lord lying unconscious on the ground. The lord decides to play a practical joke on Sly; he takes the unconscious tinker to his home, dresses him like a gentleman, and orders his servants to treat him as if he has been insane for many years, but has just now recovered. When Sly awakens, the lord introduces him to his "wife," the lord's page dressed as a woman, and announces the evening's entertainment: a play. This introductory episode is structured as a framing plot, a dramatic structure in which another drama is enclosed. Christopher Sly, onstage, watches the traveling company of players perform *The Taming of the Shrew*. At the close of act 1, scene 1, Sly and his "wife" exchange brief comments on the play they are watching. While Sly probably remains onstage for the second scene of act 1, he speaks no more lines, and the audience shifts its attention to the players' performance.

Act 1 reveals the dramatic situation and sets in motion the action of the play. In scene 1 Lucentio and his servant Tranio arrive in Padua and observe a scene: Signor Baptista explains to the youthful Hortensio and the elderly Gremio that he will not allow them to court his younger daughter, Bianca, until his elder daughter, Kate, is married. Hortensio and Gremio therefore agree to find a husband for the notorious shrew Kate, and meanwhile devise plans to court Bianca secretly. Lucentio, who has fallen in love at first sight with Bianca while watching this scene, decides to disguise himself as a scholar so that he can court Bianca secretly in the guise of a tutor; Tranio will pretend to be Lucentio and will negotiate publicly with Baptista for Bianca's hand in marriage. In act 1, scene 2, Petruchio arrives at the home of his friend Hortensio and announces his plan to find a rich wife. Hortensio suggests that he court Kate, and he agrees to do so.

Act 2 and the first scene of act 3 focus on public and private marriage negotiations. Petruchio presents himself to Baptista as a suitor for Kate and arranges a marriage agreement, contingent on Kate's acceptance. Petruchio and Kate then engage in a private battle of wits, which concludes with Petruchio's public announcement that Kate has agreed to marry him. Kate's protest is silenced. Counterpointing Petruchio's courtship are the public and private negotiations for Bianca's hand in marriage. Tranio, pretending to be Lucentio, and old Gremio bid against each other for Baptista's consent, while Lucentio, disguised as a poetry tutor, and Hortensio, disguised as a music tutor, privately woo Bianca. Baptista accepts Lucentio's bid, contingent on the arrival of his father, Vincentio, to substantiate his claim of a vast fortune.

In the center of the play, act 3, scene 2, Petruchio and Kate are married. Petruchio arrives very late for the wedding, dressed in outrageous, ragged clothes. He behaves obnoxiously at the wedding and defies social custom by leaving directly after the ceremony with Kate. Kate is furious, but Petruchio carries her off in spite of her resistance.

Act 4 alternates between scenes focused on Kate and Petruchio's first week of marriage and scenes focused on Tranio's plan to find a stand-in for Lucentio's father, an imposter who will verify the claim to vast wealth that Tranio, pretending to be Lucentio, has made to win Bianca's hand. Scenes 1, 3, and

5 show us Petruchio's taming method on the road from Padua to his country house, at the house, and on the road back to Padua for Bianca's wedding. Petruchio likens his method to taming a wild falcon and insists that Kate must stop contradicting him if she wishes to return to Padua for Bianca's wedding. On the road back to Padua, Kate says she will agree to whatever Petruchio says, even to the point of addressing an elderly man as though he were a young girl. The old man later identifies himself as Lucentio's father, Vincentio. In scenes 2 and 4, Tranio convinces a pedant to pose as Lucentio's father and to sign a marriage contract with Baptista. Hortensio decides to marry a rich widow.

The final act opens with the secret marriage of Bianca and Lucentio. Petruchio and Kate arrive in Padua shortly after and lead Vincentio to Lucentio's house. They watch as Vincentio argues with the pedant, who is posing as Vincentio, and with Tranio, who is posing as Lucentio. Just as the real Vincentio is about to be arrested as an imposter, Lucentio and Bianca arrive, confess their secret marriage, and explain what has happened. Baptista and Vincentio forgive Bianca and Lucentio and all join together for Bianca's wedding banquet. In the final scene of the play the three new husbands, Petruchio, Lucentio, and Hortensio bet on whose wife is most obedient. Petruchio wins; Kate lectures the others on the virtues of submissiveness, and Petruchio, impressed, carries her off to bed as the others marvel at the taming of the shrew.

CHAPTER 1

The Structure and Characters of *The Taming of the Shrew*

The Structure of *The Taming of the Shrew*

David Bevington

University of Chicago professor David Bevington is the author of several book-length studies of medieval, Tudor, and Shakespearean drama and the editor of *The Complete Works of Shakespeare*. In this introduction to *The Taming of the Shrew*, Bevington specifies the basic structure of the play. He explains the play begins with an Induction, an introductory episode that serves as a prologue to the work that follows. The Induction also acts as a "framing plot," a dramatic structure in which another drama is enclosed. The audience watches Sly, who is onstage watching a play called *The Taming of the Shrew*.

The main plot of the drama Sly is watching focuses on a "battle of the sexes" courtship between Kate, the shrew of the title, and Petruchio, the shrew-tamer. In their witty war of words, Kate tests Petruchio's sincerity and Petruchio tests Kate's patience. The taming works, Bevington argues, because Petruchio insists on what Kate really desires: "a well-defined relationship tempered by mutual respect and love."

Like his other early comedies, *The Taming of the Shrew* (c. 1592–1594) looks forward to Shakespeare's mature comic drama in several ways. By skillfully juxtaposing two plots and an induction, or framing plot, it offers contrasting views on the battle of the sexes. This debate on the nature of the love relationship will continue through many later comedies. The play also adroitly manipulates the device of mistaken identity, as in *The Comedy of Errors*, inverting appearance and reality, dream and waking, and the master-servant relationship in order to create a transformed Saturnalian world anticipating that of *A Midsummer Night's Dream* and *Twelfth Night*.

Excerpted from *William Shakespeare: Four Comedies*, by David Bevington, editor. Copyright ©1988 by David Bevington (Introduction and Notes). Used by permission of Bantam Books, a division of Random House, Inc.

THE SLY INDUCTION

The Induction sets up the theme of illusion, using an old motif known as "The Sleeper Awakened" (as found for example in *The Arabian Nights).* This device frames the main action of the play, giving to it an added perspective. *The Taming of the Shrew* purports in fact to be a play within a play, an entertainment devised by a witty nobleman as a practical joke on a drunken tinker, Christopher Sly. The jest is to convince Sly that he is not Sly at all, but an aristocrat suffering delusions. Outlandishly dressed in new finery, Sly is invited to witness a play from the gallery over the stage. In a rendition called *The Taming of a Shrew* (printed in 1594 and now generally thought to be taken from an earlier version of Shakespeare's play, employing a good deal of conscious originality along with some literary borrowing and even plagiarism), the framing plot concludes by actually putting Sly back out on the street in front of the ale-house where he was found. He awakes, recalls the play as a dream, and proposes to put the vision to good use by taming his own wife. Whether this ending reflects an epilogue now lost from the text of Shakespeare's play cannot be said, but it does reinforce the idea of the play as Sly's fantasy. Like Puck at the end of *A Midsummer Night's Dream,* urging us to dismiss what we have seen as the product of our own slumbering, Sly continually reminds us that the play is only an illusion or shadow.

With repeated daring, Shakespeare calls attention to the contrived nature of his artifact, the play. When, for example, Sly is finally convinced that he is in fact a noble lord recovering from madness and lustily proposes to hasten off to bed with his long-neglected wife, we are comically aware that the "wife" is an impostor, a young page in disguise. Yet this counterfeiting of roles is no more unreal than the employment of Elizabethan boy-actors for the parts of Katharina and Bianca in the "real" play. As we watch Sly watching a play, levels of meaning interplay in this evocative fashion. Again, the paintings offered to Sly by his new attendants call attention to art's ability to confound illusion and reality. In one painting, Cytherea is hidden by reeds "Which seem to move and wanton with her breath / Even as the waving sedges play wi' th' wind," and in another painting Io appears "As lively painted as the deed was done." Sly's function, then, is that of the naive observer who inverts illusion and reality in his mind, concluding that his whole previous life of tinkers and ale-houses and Cicely Hackets has been unreal. As his attendants explain to him, "These fifteen years you have been in a dream, / Or when you waked, so waked as if you slept." We as audience laugh at Sly's naiveté, and yet we too are moved and even transformed by an artistic vision that we know to be illusory.

Like Sly, many characters in the main action of the play are persuaded, or nearly persuaded, to be what they are not. Lucentio and Tranio exchange roles of master and servant. Bianca's supposed tutors are in fact her wooers, using their lessons to disguise messages of love. Katharina is prevailed upon by her husband, Petruchio, to declare that the sun is the moon and that an old gentleman (Vincentio) is a fair young maiden. Vincentio is publicly informed that he is an impostor, and that the "real" Vincentio (the Pedant) is at that very moment looking at him out of the window of his son Lucentio's house. This last ruse does not fool the real Vincentio, but it nearly succeeds in fooling everyone else. Baptista Minola is about to commit Vincentio to jail for the infamous slander of asserting that the supposed Lucentio is only a servant in disguise. Vincentio, as the newly arrived stranger, is able to see matters as they really are; but the dwellers of Padua have grown so accustomed to the mad and improbable fictions of their life that they are not easily awakened to reality.

THE ROMANTIC SUBPLOT

Shakespeare multiplies these devices of illusion by combining two entirely distinct plots, each concerned at least in part with the comic inversion of appearance and reality: the shrew-taming plot involving Petruchio and Kate, and the more conventional romantic plot involving Lucentio and Bianca. The latter plot is derived from the *Supposes* of George Gascoigne, a play first presented at Gray's Inn in 1566 as translated from Ariosto's neoclassical comedy *I Suppositi*, 1509. (Ariosto's work in turn was based upon Terence's *Eunuchus* and Plautus' *Captivi*.) The "Supposes" are mistaken identities or misunderstandings, the kind of hilarious farcical mix-ups Shakespeare had already experimented with in *The Comedy of Errors*. Shakespeare has, as usual, both romanticized his source and moralized it in a characteristically English way. The heroine, who in the Roman comedy of Plautus and Terence would have been a courtesan, and who in *Supposes* is made pregnant by her clandestine lover, remains thoroughly chaste in Shake-speare's comedy. Consequently she has no need for a pan-der, or go-between, such as the bawdy duenna, or nurse, of *Supposes*. The satire directed at the heroine's unwelcome old wooer is far less savage than in *Supposes*, where the "pan-taloon," Dr. Cleander, is a villainously corrupt lawyer epito-mizing the depravity of "respectable" society. Despite Shake-speare's modifications, however, the basic plot remains an effort to foil parental authority. The young lovers, choosing each other for romantic reasons, must fend off the material-istic calculations of their parents.

In a stock situation of this sort, the character types are also conventional. Gremio, the aged wealthy wooer, is actually la-beled a "pantaloon" in the text to stress his neoclassical an-cestry. (Lean and foolish old wooers of this sort were cus-tomarily dressed in pantaloons, slippers, and spectacles on the Italian stage.) Gremio is typically "the graybeard," and Baptista Minola is "the narrow prying father." Even though Shakespeare renders these characters far less unattractive than in *Supposes*, their worldly behavior still invites reprisal from the young. Since Baptista Minola insists on selling his daughter Bianca to the highest bidder, it is fitting that her wealthiest suitor (the supposed Lucentio) should turn out in the end to be a penniless servant (Tranio) disguised as a man of affluence and position. In his traditional role as the clever servant of neoclassical comedy, Tranio skillfully apes the mannerisms of respectable society. He can deal in the mere surfaces, clothes or reputation, out of which a man's social importance is created, and can even furnish himself with a rich father. Gremio and Baptista deserve to be foiled because they accept the illusion of respectability as real.

Even the romantic lovers of this borrowed plot are largely conventional. To be sure, Shakespeare emphasizes their vir-tuous qualities and their sincerity. He adds Hortensio (not in *Supposes*) to provide Lucentio with a genuine, if foolish, ri-val and Bianca with two wooers closer to her age than old Gremio. Lucentio and Bianca deserve their romantic tri-umph; they are self-possessed, witty, and steadfast to each other. Yet we know very little about them, nor have they seen deeply into each other. Lucentio's love talk is laden with con-ventional images in praise of Bianca's dark eyes and scarlet lips. At the play's end, he discovers, to his surprise, that she can be willful, even disobedient. Has her appearance of virtue concealed something from him and from us? Because the relationship between these lovers is superficial, they are appropriately destined to a superficial marriage as well. The passive Bianca becomes the proud and defiant wife.

THE SHREW-TAMING PLOT

By contrast, Petruchio and Kate are the more interesting lovers, whose courtship involves mutual self-discovery. Admittedly, we must not overstate the case. Especially at first, these lovers are also stock types: the shrew tamer and his proverbially shrewish wife. Although Shakespeare seems not to have used any single source for this plot, he was well acquainted with crude misogynistic stories demonstrating the need for putting women in their place. In a ballad called *A Merry Jest of a Shrewd and Curst Wife Lapped in Morel's Skin* (printed c. 1550), for example, the husband tames his shrewish spouse by flaying her bloody with birch rods and then wrapping her in the freshly salted skin of a plow horse named Morel. (This shrewish wife, like Kate, has an obedient and gentle younger sister who is their father's favorite.) Other features of Shakespeare's plot can be found in similar tales: the tailor scolded for devising a gown of outlandish fashion (Gerard Legh's *Accidence of Armory,* 1562), the wife obliged to agree with her husband's assertion of some patent falsehood (Don Juan Manuel's *El Conde Lucanor,* 1335), and the three husbands' wager on their wives' obedience (*The Book of the Knight of La Tour-Landry,* printed 1484). In the raw spirit of this sexist tradition, so unlike the refined Italianate sentiment of his other plot, Shakespeare introduces Petruchio as a man of reckless bravado who is ready to marry the ugliest or sharpest-tongued woman alive so long as she is rich. However much he may later be attracted by Kate's fiery spirit, his first attraction to her is crassly financial. Kate is, moreover, a thoroughly disagreeable young woman at first, described by those who know her as "intolerable curst / And shrewd, and froward" and aggressive in her bullying of Bianca. She and Petruchio meet as grotesque comic counterparts. At the play's end, the traditional pattern of male dominance and female acquiescence is still prominent. Kate achieves peace only by yielding to a socially ordained patriarchal framework in which a husband is the princely ruler of his wife.

Within this male-oriented frame of reference, however,

Petruchio and Kate are surprisingly like Benedick and Beatrice of *Much Ado about Nothing*. Petruchio, for all his rant, is increasingly drawn to Kate by her spirit. As wit-combatants they are worthy of each other's enmity—or love. No one else in the play is a fit match for either of them. Kate too is attracted to Petruchio, despite her war of words. Her guise of hostility is part defensive protection, part testing of his sincerity. If she is contemptuous of the wooers she has seen till now, she has good reason to be. We share her condescension toward the aged Gremio or the laughably inept Hortensio. She rightly fears that her father wishes to dispose of her so that he may auction off Bianca to the wealthiest competitor. Kate's jaded view of such marriage brokering is entirely defensible. Not surprisingly she first views Petruchio, whose professed intentions are far from reassuring, as another mere adventurer in love. She is impressed by his "line" in wooing her, but needs to test his constancy and sincerity. Possibly she is prepared to accept the prevailing Elizabethan view of marriage, with its dominant role for the husband, but only if she can choose a man deserving of her respect. She puts down most men with a shrewish manner that challenges their very masculinity; Petruchio is the first to be man enough to "board" her. Kate's rejection of men does not leave her very happy, however genuine her disdain is for most of those who come to woo. Petruchio's "schooling" is therefore curative. Having wooed and partly won her, he tests her with his late arrival at the marriage, his unconventional dress, and his crossing all her desires. In this display of willfulness, he shows her an ugly picture of what she herself is like. Most of all, however, he succeeds because he insists on what she too desires: a well-defined relationship tempered by mutual respect and love. Kate is visibly a more contented person at the play's end. Her closing speech, with its fine blend of irony and self-conscious hyperbole, together with its seriousness of concern, expresses beautifully the way in which Kate's independence of spirit and her newfound acceptance of a domestic role are successfully fused.

Plays and Play-Making in *The Taming of the Shrew*

J. Dennis Huston

Author of *Shakespeare's Comedies of Play*, J. Dennis Huston explores in this article the implications of "the hall of mirrors" structure of *The Taming of the Shrew*. By creating a series of plays within plays, Shakespeare "upsets our sense of the order of things" and encourages the audience to participate in the drama. Huston compares the Christopher Sly introductory episode to the main plot, Petruchio's taming of Kate, and claims that the Lord who discovers the unconscious Sly and Petruchio are both directors of plays. The Lord plots to make Sly believe he is a gentleman, and Petruchio plays havoc with Kate's expectations in order to free her from the limited role of a shrew. Huston also explores the similarities between Shakespeare and Petruchio by arguing that both the playwright and Petruchio invite audience participation in play. Petruchio encourages Kate to escape clichéd, mechanical, puppetlike responses and enter the freedom of play; likewise, Shakespeare encourages the audience to actively "join with the author in his play of mind."

The Induction starts with an enormous explosion of energy. From offstage we hear sounds of a quarrel, and perhaps of glass breaking, and then Sly reels across the stage in drunken flight from the enraged Hostess. He promises violence, and she no doubt inflicts it, as they argue about his bill and trade insults until she realizes she can do nothing to control the drunken rogue and runs off to fetch the law. Sly, too drunk to care about her beatings or threats, hurls a senseless challenge after her and then passes out. The brief

Excerpted from "'To Make a Puppet': Play and Playmaking in *The Taming of the Shrew*," by J. Dennis Huston, in *Shakespeare Studies*, vol. 9, edited by J. Leeds Barroll III. Copyright ©1976 by The Council for Research in the Renaissance. Published by Burt Franklin and Co. Reprinted by permission of the author.

episode is a theatrical *tour de force* [feat of strength]; there has never been a beginning quite like it on the English stage before, and there will not be one to overgo it in pure physical energy until the spectacular opening scene of *The Alchemist* more than fifteen years later. For here Shakespeare has begun in medias res with a vengeance.

The theater audience, noisily settling into place to watch a comedy, knows what to expect. However, Shakespeare dispels that self-assurance. He presents not traditional dramatic exposition, not a Prologue or an Induction giving a clear and careful summary of problems at hand, but an explosion. And then, almost as suddenly as this episode began—and before we really know what it is about—it is over, and the stage is quiet again so that the audience can have the kind of beginning it expected in the first place: enter a lord and his servants at leisure. After disruption, a return to normalcy. But now the normalcy does not altogether satisfy us, because we wonder about the apparently abandoned beginning. Why is what was so spectacularly begun so quickly over? When is the thirdborough going to come? Why has Shakespeare left Sly on stage? Is it so that the Lord can discover him? Why doesn't the Lord notice him? What will he *do* with Sly if he does see him? The Lord talks on about his hounds, and we wait impatiently for something to happen.

In the process we may also become vaguely aware of themes from the earlier episode repeated in different tones. There is talk of money and an argument which, though it is nothing like Sly's fight with the Hostess, still provokes an insult: "Thou art a fool." We hear again of "cold," but now the reference is to a scent in the hunt. This dramatic world provides a marked contrast to the disordered one we first saw, but something of that first world lingers here still, not only in the heaped figure at the edge of the stage but also in the distant echoes of the language. Then the worlds collide. The Lord stumbles upon Sly, and like the Hostess earlier, he must decide what to do with him. She tried to beat Sly into shape and failed, leaving behind her on the stage a mass of indeterminate, subhuman form. The Lord at first tries his art at shaping this mass into a neatly ordered exemplum: "Grim death, how foul and loathsome is thine image!" But soon he sees more interesting and complex possibilities for form in the shapeless mound before him—if he has but art enough. He will create Sly anew in his own image, raising him up to life as a lord:

> Carry him gently to my fairest chamber
> And hang it round with all my wanton pictures:
> Balm his foul head in warm distilled waters
> And burn sweet wood to make the lodging sweet:
> Procure me music ready when he wakes,
> To make a dulcet and a heavenly sound;
> And if he chance to speak, be ready straight
> And with a low submissive reverence
> Say 'What is it your honour will command?'
> .   .   .   .   .
> Some one be ready with a costly suit
> And ask him what apparel he will wear.

What is happening here is that the creative impulse is taking hold of the Lord and he is becoming a playwright, imagining the details of scene, costume, and even dialogue. What is also happening is that Shakespeare is disorienting his audience again. As we expected, he has brought his Lord and Sly together so that the action of the play can begin, but the action that then begins is the action of imagining the beginning of a play. And that play, its author tells us, is a "jest." We are lost in the funhouse sure. We must, however, get more lost before we can be found. Shakespeare has barely started us on our journey through this dramatic hall of mirrors.

A HALL OF MIRRORS

The plot to make a lord of Sly is no sooner begun than it too is interrupted. A trumpet sounds the arrival of someone of note, and the Lord, perhaps still inclining to the role of playwright, imagines an identity and purpose for the visitor: "Belike, some noble gentleman that means, / Travelling some journey, to repose him here." The hypothesis is logical enough, and perhaps Shakespeare is just adding a naturalistic detail to his characterization of the Lord; we all fantasize about visitors at our doors. But this fantasy also repeats a pattern we have noted before in the scene: it arouses the audience's expectations about the form Shakespeare's play will take, apparently only to frustrate those expectations. One conventional way to begin the action of a comedy, particularly of a Shakespearean comedy, is with the arrival of an outsider or group of outsiders . . . who disrupt things as they are. For a fleeting moment Shakespeare here offers us such a beginning and then takes it away. The imagined noble gentleman melts into thin air; the men who enter before us are merely players. . . .

The players arouse our interest, not so much because of what they do—the Lord's discussion with them of a play they have acted in the past seems designed, like his earlier talk about the worth of his hounds, to allow us the freedom to pay only casual attention—but because of what they are. Everywhere in this Induction we encounter forms of play and figures of players. Sly, determined to "let the world slide," has drunk away the workaday realm of cares and law, and now he can at least play at being someone more important than a beggarly tinker: "the Slys are no rogues; look in the chronicles; we came in with Richard Conqueror." The Lord too avoids a world of workaday, passing his days in sport and filling his evening with "pastime passing excellent." He converts his bedchamber into a kind of theater and gives his servants instructions in the art of staging a play. But hardly has he done so when he is interrupted by the fortuitous arrival of "real" players—"real" both by the standards of his world and the audience's, though for the audience this "reality" is double-imaged, since the players are "really" players playing players. In this hall of mirrors that is the Induction we find another hall of mirrors reflecting other halls of mirrors as far as we can see: Shakespeare begins a play, which is then apparently rebegun as a more conventional play, in which a Lord decides to stage a play, but he is interrupted by a group of players, who themselves come to offer service in the form of a play to this Lord, who talks with them about yet another play, which they have acted in the past but which they are not going to present this evening, when a player-lord will observe their performance of a play staged after the "real" Lord and his servants have played out their play with the player-lord, who will sleep through the play which Shakespeare, himself playing through this mind-boggling series of false starts, will ultimately present to *his* audience!

Shakespeare's purposes here are almost as complex as his method. First, he is, like his surrogate figure the Lord, merely playing—recording for his audience the almost unbounded joy of a young man doing something whose possibilities are commensurate with his enormous energies. Such an attitude is also characteristic of Petruchio, whose distinguishing quality is his love of play and essential joie de vivre [joy of living]. This quality of life he is eventually to impart to Kate, who has to learn to direct her own enormous energies outward into varieties of spontaneous play instead of recalcitrantly forcing them into the narrowly confining roles society would impose on her. Of necessity, she will still have to play roles and harness her volatile energies within the compass of forms, some of them tyrannically arbitrary—"be it moon, or sun, or what you please"—but she will have learned that since playing roles is an unavoidable consequence of the human condition, the very humanness of that condition is determined by the quality and intensity of the play as play. . . .

PLAYS UPSET ORDER

Why does Shakespeare keep taking us deeper into the illusive realm of plays within plays? Why does he play such havoc with our expectations about how this play will begin? Gradually we recognize that Shakespeare is wielding over us some of the same powers that the Lord wields over Sly: he is presenting us with a play which upsets our sense of the order of things. But the real purpose of suggesting such a correspondence may be to make us aware of differences. We would hope that we are a more receptive audience than Sly and that Shakespeare is doing more than merely playing a joke on us. Then, too, our consciousness of manipulated response and thwarted expectations may increase our sensitivity to such problems when they become central themes in the shrew-taming plot. There Kate's responses are at first destructively manipulated by a society which judges her—and at least has partly made her—an alien. Baptista's initial exit in Act I, scene i, when he conspicuously leaves Kate behind because he has "more to commune with Bianca" is surely an emblematic statement of Kate's exclusion from the family unit. And a similar condition of isolation from society as a whole is suggested by the way characters talk derisively about Kate in her presence, almost as if she were not there at all. But if society isolates Kate by manipulating her, Petruchio integrates her by manipulation.

The way he manipulates her is to frustrate her expectations continually. He comes courting with praise for her beauty and mildness when everyone else has called her a plain shrew; he stands unshaken, even apparently unnoticing, against her attacks when everyone else has fled her wrath in terror; he announces he will marry her when everyone else has proclaimed her unmarriageable. But when he has won Kate's hand in this madcap manner, Petruchio has only begun to play havoc with her expectations. Greater violence is to follow—at the wedding, on the journey from home, at his country house, on the road back to Padua, and even at the final wedding feast. By then, however, Kate will have learned her lesson: that society's conventions are imprisoning not so much because they force inchoate human energies and desires into limiting forms—a necessary condition of any social intercourse—but because they can so easily *replace* those energies and desires. Forms may abide where there is no longer feeling, indeed, may even drive out feeling. . . .

Conventions Replace Feelings

Love may be reduced to solicitous public concern or to patently possessive favoritism, as it is with Baptista for his daughters. Or it may become tantalizing flirtation, as with Bianca; or self-generated fantasizing, as with Lucentio; or plain and practical self-interest, as with Hortensio. It may even appear as comically misshapen greed, as with Gremio. What matters is not the form to which it has been reduced but the act of reduction itself. For in a world ruled, not served, by convention, energies once spontaneously felt either dissolve into cliché—Baptista talking like a loving father about his daughters, Lucentio pining after Bianca in the language of a Renaissance sonneteer, Hortensio fitting his love poetry to the formula of a gamut—or lock themselves into obsessive, repetitive behavior—Grumio's recurrent concern for food and sex, Grumio's instinctive twitch toward his money bag, Kate's repeated attempts to beat others into submission. In such a world man is threatened ultimately by dehumanization: he can act either formulaically in cliché or mechanically in obsession, but he cannot *act* in the true philosophical or theatrical sense of the word because he can no longer feel. All spontaneity, all play disappears.

"The Puppet" Awakens and Lives

"Belike you mean to make a puppet of me," Kate cries in frustration when Petruchio will not let her have the gown the tailor has delivered. In this judgment of Petruchio's purposes Kate is both right and wrong. Yes, Petruchio is here playing puppet-master with Kate, making her do exactly what he wants. But he makes a puppet of her so that she may be delivered from her woodenness of response, from her imprisonment in a tree: in nonhuman nature. When she first meets Petruchio, Kate is a kind of puppet—hard, grotesquely limited both in feeling and action, manipulated by a force she cannot control. But she does not realize she is puppet-like. In fact, she obstinately argues to the contrary:

> Why, and I trust I may go too, may I not?
> What, shall I be appointed hours; as though, belike,
> I knew not what to take, and what to leave, ha?

Manipulated by society, family, and her own uncontrollable emotions, Kate cannot see what she is. Petruchio, however, makes his manipulation of Kate obvious; he makes her see that she has become a puppet so that, recognizing her condition, she may alter it, may escape from the bondage of a mechanical existence into the freedom of human form and play. That freedom is, it is important to note, not absolute. All man's world is but a stage and he is merely a player, an actor fleshing out a variety of roles. But compared to a puppet, he is a full and fine thing indeed. Petruchio calls Kate out of the woodenness of the puppet show into the human theater of play. Her answer is, shortly, to command stage-center.

And what Petruchio does to Kate, Shakespeare does to his audience in the Induction. He writes as if he means to make a puppet out of this audience, manipulating its responses in sudden and arbitrary ways, jerking it first one way and then another. But also like Petruchio, he calls attention to his actions by carrying them to extremes. In the process he wakens the audience to perception. He shows it that the theater it sits in, where actors play parts assigned to them, is just another form of the theater it daily lives in: "do I dream? or have I dream'd till now?" And then he invites the audience to join with him in the act of playing: its role will be, of course—audience. The role is not to be taken lightly. Mere polite attention will not serve, for that is not *playing* the role of audience; it is slipping woodenly into convention, which for Shakespeare is little better behavior at a play than nodding drunkenly into sleep. "My lord, you nod; you do not mind the play," a servingman tells Sly, but the words are addressed also to the audience of Shakespeare's play. For if this audience does not "mind" the play, does not bring to it all energies and faculties of mind in an effort to join with the author in his play of mind, then it is no better an audience than Sly, and perhaps in the theater of its world awaits no better fate than he—unaccountably cast into oblivion by the playwright who first breathed the magic of life into him.

The Female Characters

Harold C. Goddard

The late Harold C. Goddard was head of the English
Department at Swarthmore College from 1909 to
1946. His two-volume study of Shakespeare's plays,
The Meaning of Shakespeare, was praised by literary
critic Mark Van Doren as "personal" and "provocative" and by Lionel Trilling as "a warm and humane
reading of Shakespeare which the student and the
general reader will find truly enlightening." In his
analysis of *The Taming of the Shrew*, Goddard challenges readers to interpret the ending of the play
shrewdly. Unlike the anonymous play, *The Taming
of a Shrew*, which ends with Christopher Sly determined to tame his wife, Shakespeare's play ends
without returning to Sly. To a shrewd reader, who
discerns the similarity between Shakespeare's sleepy
Sly (who only thinks he is a lord) and Petruchio,
Shakespeare's ending may suggest that both Sly and
Petruchio are about to experience an "awakening"—
when their respective plays are over, both may find
their "wives" less obedient than they appear. As
every woman knows, Goddard claims, "the woman
can lord it over the man so long as she allows him to
think he is lording it over her."

[Shakespeare] was fond of under- and overmeanings he
could not have expected his audience as a whole to get. But
it is *The Taming of the Shrew* that is possibly the most striking example among his early works of his love of so contriv-
ing a play that it should mean, to those who might choose to
take it so, the precise opposite of what he knew it would
mean to the multitude. For surely the most psychologically
sound as well as the most delightful way of taking *The Taming of the Shrew* is the topsy-turvy one. Kate, in that case, is
no shrew at all except in the most superficial sense. Bianca,

on the other hand, is just what her sister is supposed to be. And the play ends with the prospect that Kate is going to be more nearly the tamer than the tamed, Petruchio more nearly the tamed than the tamer, though his wife naturally will keep the true situation under cover. So taken, the play is an early version of *What Every Woman Knows*—what every woman knows being, of course, that the woman can lord it over the man so long as she allows him to think he is lording it over her. This interpretation has the advantage of bringing the play into line with all the other Comedies in which Shakespeare gives a distinct edge to his heroine. Otherwise it is an unaccountable exception and regresses to the wholly un-Shakespearean doctrine of male superiority, a view which there is not the slightest evidence elsewhere Shakespeare ever held.

KATE AND BIANCA ARE NOT WHAT THEY APPEAR

We must never for a moment allow ourselves to forget that *The Taming of the Shrew* is a play within a play, an interlude put on by a company of strolling players at the house of a great lord for the gulling of Christopher Sly, the drunken tinker, and thereby for the double entertainment of the audience. For the sake of throwing the picture into strong relief against the frame . . . the play within the play is given a simplification and exaggeration that bring its main plot to the edge of farce, while its minor plot, the story of Bianca's wooers, goes quite over that edge. But, even allowing for this, the psychology of the Katharine-Petruchio plot is remarkably realistic. It is even "modern" in its psychoanalytical implications. It is based on the familiar situation of the favorite child. Baptista is a family tyrant and Bianca is his favorite daughter. She has to the casual eye all the outer marks of modesty and sweetness, but to a discerning one all the inner marks of a spoiled pet, remade, if not originally made, in her father's image. One line is enough to give us her measure. When in the wager scene at the end her husband tells her that her failure to come at his entreaty has cost him a hundred crowns,

> The more fool you for laying on my duty,

she blurts out. What a light that casts back over her previous "sweetness" before she has caught her man! The rest of her role amply supports this interpretation, as do the hundreds of Biancas—who are not as white as they are painted—in real life.

Apart from the irony and the effective contrast so obtained, there is everything to indicate that Kate's shrewishness is superficial, not ingrained or congenital. It is the inevitable result of her father's gross partiality toward her sister and neglect of herself, plus the repercussions that his attitude has produced on Bianca and almost everyone else in the region. Kate has heard herself blamed, and her sister praised at her expense, to a point where even a worm would turn. And Kate is no worm. If her sister is a spoiled child, Kate is a cross child who is starved for love. She craves it as a man in a desert craves water, without understanding, as he does, what is the matter. And though we have to allow for the obvious exaggeration of farce in his extreme antics, Petruchio's procedure at bottom shows insight, understanding, and even love. Those actors who equip him with a whip miss Shakespeare's man entirely. In principle, if not in the rougher details, he employs just the right method in the circumstances, and the end amply justifies his means.

It is obvious that his boast at the outset of purely mercenary motives for marrying is partly just big talk—at any rate the dowry soon becomes quite subsidiary to Kate herself and the game of taming her. In retrospect it seems to have been something like love at first sight on both sides, though not recognized as such at the time. Whatever we think of Petruchio's pranks in the scenes where farce and comedy get mixed, there is no quarreling with his instinctive sense of how in general Kate ought to be handled. When a small child is irritable and cross, the thing to do is not to reason, still less to pity or pamper, or even to be just kind and understanding in the ordinary sense. The thing to do is to take the child captive. A vigorous body and will, combined with good humor and a love that is not expressed in words but that makes itself felt by a sort of magnetic communication, will sweep the child off his feet, carry him away, and transform him almost miraculously back into his natural self. Anyone who does not know that knows mighty little about children. This is precisely what Petruchio does to Kate (and what Shakespeare does to his audience in this play). She is dying for affection. He keeps calling her his sweet and lovely Kate. What if he is ironical to begin with! The words just of themselves are manna to her soul, and her intuition tells her that, whether he knows it or not, he really means them. And indeed Kate is lovely and sweet by nature. (She is worth a bale of Biancas.) What girl would not like to be told, as Petruchio tells her, that she sings as sweetly as a nightingale and has a countenance like morning roses washed with dew? She knows by a perfectly sound instinct that he could never have thought up such lovely similes to be sarcastic with if he considered her nothing but a shrew. There is a poet within him that her beauty has elicited. What wonder that she weeps when the poet fails to appear for the wedding! It is not just humiliation. It is disappointed love.

And Kate is intelligent too. She is a shrewd "shrew." You can put your finger on the very moment when it dawns on her that if she will just fall in with her husband's absurdest whim, accept his maddest perversion of the truth as truth, she can take the wind completely out of his sails, deprive his weapon of its power, even turn it against him—tame him in his own humor. Not that she really wants to tame him, for she loves him dearly, as the delightful little scene in the street so amply proves, where he begs a kiss, begs, be it noted, not demands. She is shy for fear they may be overseen, but finally relents and consents.

KATH.:   Husband, let's follow, to see the end of this ado.
PET.:   First kiss me, Kate, and we will.
KATH.:   What! in the midst of the street?
PET.:   What! art thou ashamed of me?
KATH.:   No, sir, God forbid; but ashamed to kiss.
PET.:   Why, then let's home again. Come, sirrah, let's away.
KATH.:   Nay, I will give thee a kiss; now pray thee, love, stay.
PET.:   Is not this well? Come, my sweet Kate.
         Better once than never, for never too late. . . .

A SHREW IS DIFFERENT FROM *THE* SHREW

In a mathematical proportion, if three of the terms are known, the fourth unknown one (x) can easily be determined. Thus, if $(a/b) = (c/x)$, it follows that $x = (bc/a)$. The poet often proceeds from the known to the unknown by a similar procedure, but unlike the mathematician he does not meticulously put the x on one side and carefully label the other side of the equation "answer." He supplies the data rather and leaves it to the reader to figure out or not, as he chooses, what follows from them. This was plainly the method Shakespeare used in relating the story of Christopher Sly to the story of Petruchio.

It is generally agreed that the Induction to *The Taming of the Shrew* is one of the most masterly bits of writing to be found anywhere in Shakespeare's earlier works. Much as the authorship of the play has been debated, no one, so far as I recall, has ever questioned the authorship of the Induction. Shakespeare evidently bestowed on it a care that indicates the importance it had in his eyes. In *The Taming of a Shrew* (whose relation to *The Taming of the Shrew* has recently been widely discussed) the purpose of the Induction with reference to the play itself is made perfectly clear by a return to Sly at the end after the play within the play is over. Christopher Sly, the drunken tinker, has a wife who is a shrew. In the play that is acted before him he watches the successful subjugation of another woman to the will of her husband, and at the end of the performance we see him starting off for home to try out on his own wife the knowledge he has just acquired. Whatever part, if any, Shakespeare had in the earlier play, why did he spoil a good point in the later one by not completing its framework, by failing to return to Sly at the end of the Petruchio play? All sorts of explanations for the artistic lapse have been conjured up, the most popular being that the last leaf of the manuscript, in which he did so return, was somehow lost or that the scene was left to the improvisation of the actors and so was never reduced to writing. But surely the editors of the *Folio* would have been aware of this and could have supplied at least a stage direction to clear things up!

I wonder if the explanation of the enigma is not a simpler and more characteristic one: that Shakespeare saw his chance for a slyer and profounder relation between the Induction and the play than in the earlier version of the story.

Sly and Petruchio Are About to Be Awakened

In the Induction to *The Taming of the Shrew*, Christopher Sly the tinker, drunk with ale, is persuaded that he is a great lord who has been the victim of an unfortunate lunacy. Petruchio, in the play which Sly witnesses (when he is not asleep), is likewise persuaded that he is a great lord—over his wife. Sly is obviously in for a rude awakening when he discovers that he is nothing but a tinker after all. Now Petruchio is a bit intoxicated himself—who can deny it?—whether with pride, love, or avarice, or some mixture of the three. Is it possible that he too is in for an awakening? Or, if Kate does not let it come to that, that *we* at least are supposed to see that he is not as great a lord over his wife as he imagined? . . . Shakespeare wants us to find things for ourselves. And in this case in particular: why explain what is as clear, when you see it, as was Poe's Purloined Letter, which was skilfully concealed precisely because it was in such plain sight all the time?

There are two little touches in the first twenty-five lines of the Induction that seem to clinch this finally, if it needs any clinching. The Lord and his huntsmen come in from hunting. They are talking of the hounds and their performances:

LORD: Saw'st thou not, boy, how Silver made it good
           At the hedge-corner, in the coldest fault?
           I would not lose the dog for twenty pound.
FIRST HUNT.: Why, Bellman is as good as he, my lord;
           He cried upon it at the merest loss,
           And twice today pick'd out the dullest scent:
           Trust me, I take him for the better dog.

Why, in what looks like a purely atmospheric passage, this double emphasis on the power to pick up a dull or cold scent? Why if not as a hint to spectators and readers to keep alert for something they might easily miss?

Shrews and Shrew-Taming

Frances E. Dolan

Frances E. Dolan is the author of *Dangerous Familiars*, a book-length study on domestic crime in sixteenth- and seventeenth-century England, and editor of a volume of Renaissance texts concerned with marriage, household authority, and violence. In this selection, Dolan explains what a shrew is in sixteenth- and seventeenth-century England, and how shrewish behavior is punished unofficially at home and by neighbors. She also distinguishes between "shrews" and "scolds." "Shrew" is a term of abuse; "scold" is a legal category of offense punishable by cucking (being strapped to a stool and repeatedly immersed in water) or the scold's bridle (which resembled a horse's bridle and sometimes had a bit to hold down the tongue).

What *is* a shrew? How does a shrew act? In the sixteenth and seventeenth centuries shrews were, first and foremost, women. The term *shrew* describes the caricature or stereotype of a bossy woman that was a familiar figure in popular culture. One important component of shrewishness was talking—talking too much, or too loudly and publicly, or too crossly for a woman. Lacking other means to express anger or redress grievances, a shrew depended on her tongue. . . . Katharine certainly wields her tongue as a weapon. Petruchio's servant Grumio fears her tongue, should she become his mistress. Baptista warns Petruchio that if he wishes to court Katharine, he must be "armed for some unhappy words."

The contrast between Katharine and Bianca is, in part, that Katharine assaults and disturbs the suitors through their ears, while Bianca pleases their eyes. As Katharine herself complains of Bianca, "Her silence flouts me, and I'll be revenged." Lucentio is guided so much by his eyes that they take the place of his ears; in Bianca's silence he claims to "see / Maid's mild behavior and sobriety"; "I saw her coral lips to move, / And with her breath she did perfume the air. / Sacred and sweet was all I saw in her." For Lucentio romantic love is not blind but deaf. He is so absorbed in gazing at Bianca that he effectively silences what little she does say.

Lucentio's admiration for Bianca's silence suggests that the most important contrast between the two sisters is that one talks and one does not. Yet the play blurs that distinction. Bianca talks more, and more assertively, as the play progresses. The play also suggests that there is more to Katharine's shrewishness than her unruly tongue. Although it is still widely assumed that shrews talked too much, the many ballads about shrewish or scolding women reveal that

---

PUNISHMENTS FOR "SCOLDS"

In this excerpt from her book, The Taming of the Shrew: Texts and Contexts, *Frances E. Dolan introduces the popular ballad, "The Cucking of a Scold." She explains the legal punishments for women convicted of being scolds, and she emphasizes the role of the community: The shaming ritual becomes a festive occasion.*

This ballad ["The Cucking of a Scold"] describes the formal, public punishment of a scold by "cucking," or dunking her in water. Unlike "shrew," a term of abuse with no legal status, "scold" (like "witch") is a legal category, describing a woman who offends against public order and peace through her speech. . . .

Cucking was not the only possible punishment for scolding, however, nor was it a community's first choice. The community might try less violent means of shaming a scold into silence (such as the cage in the ballad). A woman sentenced to cucking might be allowed to pay a fine instead, or she might be warned that cucking would follow a second offense. Also, attempts were made to ensure that the punishment was not excessively severe or fatal. Such caution was necessary since cucking could lead to drowning; the punishment was dangerous and frightening as well as humiliating. Bridles, usually made of metal, either covered the mouth or inserted a prong (or brank) to hold down the tongue; thus, they treated the offending woman as an unruly animal. . . .

This display of the offending woman, like the cage or the pa-

women were labeled as shrews for a variety of disorderly behaviors. According to these ballads, shrews force men to do "women's work"; they beat and humiliate their husbands; they take lovers; they refuse to have sex with their husbands or blame their husbands for being sexually useless; they drink and frequent alehouses; and they scold. But most of all, they strive for mastery. . . .

A shrew, then, is not just a talkative woman; she is a woman refusing to submit to a man's authority and aggressively asserting her independence. Since English culture at this time associated self-assertion, independence, and "mastery" with masculinity, many texts depicted such women (especially married women) as usurping men's rights and privileges, rather than as claiming their own. Assertive women were imagined to overturn the existing hierarchy

rade described in "The Cucking of a Scold," suggests that shame was a crucial part of all punishments of scolds, as it was of many early modern punishments. Since shame entailed exposure to community ridicule and censure, community members were more than witnesses of these punishments; they were crucial participants.

As a result, the punishments of scolds reveal how the history of violence, crime, and punishment and the history of festivity and popular culture intersect. Rather than decide that the cucking stool and the bridle belong in one history or the other, it is most useful to consider them as evidence of both. Which emphasis looms as the most significant depends on which participant you consider—the offending woman at the center of the ceremony, or her community. The quasi-military parade to the pond and the ritual cucking of the scold described in this ballad are clearly a festive occasion for her community, if not for her: "For joy the people skipped." Describing this occasion through jaunty exaggeration, the ballad creates subsequent occasions for mirth at an assertive woman's discomfiture; each performance—especially if many singers joined in on the chorus—would be another festive occasion at the scold's expense. Of course, some witnesses of these proceedings, or audiences of the ballad, might have dissented from the revelry and objected vocally or silently. But such responses are not recorded.

Frances E. Dolan, ed., The Taming of the Shrew: *Texts and Contexts.* New York: Bedford Books of St. Martin's Press, 1996.

that placed men above women, thus making them "women on top." Any assertion of themselves was thus construed as taking something away from their husbands, as, for instance, wresting away the one pair of breeches in the family and insisting on wearing them. The possible solution of getting another pair of breeches is never imagined; instead, husband and wife must fight over that one pair. . . . It is not simply how much Katharine talks that marks her as a shrew. Indeed, she does not talk more than many of the other characters; in the first scene she has only thirteen lines, all of them in response to provocation. Nor is it even what she says. Instead, Katharine troubles and threatens other characters through a constellation of self-assertions.

SHREW-TAMING

Shrewish behavior provoked various punishments, official and unofficial. Women might be brought into court under the charge of being "scolds." This was largely a female offense, although men were occasionally presented to authorities for it. Scolding upset class as well as gender hierarchies; those women charged with scolding were usually of low status and had offended against those of equal or superior status. The punishments exacted by the community were painful, frightening, and humiliating. An offender might be forced to wear a sharp, embarrassing "scold's bridle" or might be "cucked," that is, strapped to a stool and dunked repeatedly in water. . . .

Women's shrewish assertions of their will might also be punished informally at home. Shrewish wives were widely presumed to provoke their husbands to violence, as popular songs reveal. . . . Domestic violence was fairly widespread and not legally prohibited; unless a husband disturbed his neighbors' peace or beat his wife to death, there was no cause to bring him to court and little chance of any action against him. Although there were no laws against wife beating, an increasing number of didactic texts sought to convince husbands to govern both themselves and their wives and to refrain from violence. In the view of these texts, the man who allows himself to be provoked to violence has lost control rather than regained it. On the other hand, while neighbors objected to husbands who endangered their wives' lives or who constantly engaged in loud, disturbing fights, they also objected to husbands who submitted to abuse from their wives and allowed a "shrew" to go unreprimanded.

If authorities were reluctant to interfere in how men ran their households (unless private conflicts tumbled out into public notice), neighbors pried into every detail of events next door or down the street. When they were dissatisfied, they might bring the couple before the church courts (which focused on regulating personal conduct). Or they might take matters into their own hands, embarrassing their neighbors into conforming to community standards. Organizing a raucous parade that acted out the upside-down state of affairs in a household in which the wife "wore the breeches," neighbors sought to shame husband and wife into resuming their places in a traditional gender hierarchy—masterful husband and submissive wife. But the effects of such shaming rituals were unpredictable. . . .

However we interpret Katharine's shrewishness, reading Shakespeare's play against other texts reveals that the play, like most other depictions of shrews, is full of resistant, disorderly self-assertions, not just outspokenness. Furthermore, the play, like most other depictions of shrews, focuses on taming, whatever we may think of that process. Indeed, the play explores what Petruchio thinks, feels, and does as a tamer more fully than it explores what Katharine thinks, feels, and does as a shrew.

Petruchio Is a Social Climber

Lynda E. Boose

Lynda E. Boose, associate professor of English and women's studies at Dartmouth College, is coeditor of *Daughters and Fathers* and the author of several essays that explore the issues of gender and family within a political and historical context. One of her most influential and provocative essays, "Scolding Brides and Bridling Scolds," compares the historical use of the "scold's bridle" with the restraining of Kate's tongue in *The Taming of the Shrew.*

In this article, Boose focuses on Petruchio's upward social mobility within the context of late-sixteenth-century changes in the use of land. Boose explains this change as a shift from the joint use of common land by lord, yeoman, and peasant for grazing livestock to exclusive ownership of land marked by fences. Generally speaking, the aristocrats and lower gentry benefited from this shift but many peasants were left landless. Some yeoman and peasants were able to rise in status, however, by marrying into the lower gentry. Boose argues that Christopher Sly represents one of the dispossessed peasants and that Petruchio exemplifies the land-poor yeoman son who determines, through marriage, to improve his social position.

Petruchio's success fulfills the fantasy of upward mobility for the Slys of the audience, Boose explains, because his marriage to Kate, a daughter of the gentry, gives him the status of husband, lord, and master. This superior status empowers him not only at home but also among other men. Ironically, Kate, who gives Petruchio this power by marrying him, loses her own claim, based on birth, to the status of gentlewoman. As a married woman she must submit to her husband; she can wear the cap and gown of a gentlewoman only if her husband decides she is appropriately submissive. Kate's social status as a gentlewoman,

Excerpted from "*The Taming of the Shrew,* Good Husbandry, and Enclosure," by Lynda E. Boose, in *Shakespeare Reread,* edited by Russ McDonald. Copyright ©1994 by Cornell University. Reprinted by permission of the publisher, Cornell University Press.

therefore, becomes contingent on her status in marriage, not at her birth.

Petruchio's success in achieving exclusive ownership of a wife is an effective cultural fantasy, Boose suggests, because it displaces historical yeoman anxiety about land and social class.

Sly, the lower-class male who has been dispossessed from all terms of husbandry, is set up as lord to a lady and husband to an estate, who sits by his lady to watch, in the story of Petruchio, a gendered model of male success. What he watches is an implicit pattern for obtaining social and financial prestige plus the domestic rewards of "peace . . . and love, and quiet life. / An awful rule and right supremacy; / And, to be short, what not, that's sweet and happy." But all of this good fortune itself depends on a husband's ability to demonstrate that he "will be master of what is [his] own," which, within the narrative of *The Shrew*, is a mastery whose demonstration lies in compelling "headstrong women" to know "what duty they do owe their lords and husbands." These two terms, "lord" and "husband," which are at the end of the play again paired as they were by Sly's "Madam Wife" in the Induction, are, of course, interchangeable cognates not in the world of male relations but only within the domestic sphere. All other venues being restricted by class and economic position, the statuses of "lord," "master," and "husband" are available to all men only through marriage. It is through Kate's public submission that Petruchio, having become a husband, becomes a lord indeed—and a "king," and "governor." And, as he reminds the disempowered Lucentio just before exiting the stage, it is Petruchio, alone among the men to have secured this entitlement, who exits "a winner."

MARRIAGE MAKES MAN MASTER

Besides acquiring a dominant position in society through women, inside the compensatory fiction that *The Shrew* offers, all men—from the Lord to the tinker, from the landed owner who produces and controls this fiction to the dispossessed vagrant who constitutes its target audience—are all bonded together by a common enemy: the shrewish female. Within that fantasy of egalitarian fraternity, distinctions of class get suspended and ultimately supplanted by the inner play's narration of woman taming. Through the comic mirror embedded in the play's conclusion, every man is made into potential lord in his own castle, confirmed in a status analogous to that of the landowner by the marriage covenant that guarantees him private husbandry over the wife/servant who is compelled to "serve, love, honor, and obey"—the wife/servant figure whom the Lord had placed next to Sly's bed as the reassuring sign of his status as an owner and the figure whose submission is literally staged in the inner play as the sign of Petruchio's public covenant with patriarchy. In the play's final scene, as all the players converge on Padua into the space of marriage celebration, the acting out of the shrew-taming scene transforms the celebration of "bridal" into a masculine arena of wager and competitive husbandry. Within this marketplace, disobedient wives, ironically enough, are by far the culture's most essential object. Like dragons to be conquered in medieval romance or maidens to be deflowered in love stories, the shrew appears in sixteenth- and seventeenth-century narratives as the test obstacle essential for positing the culture's terms for male dominance not only over women but over other men as well. Compelled during this era into an imaginatively heightened existence, the disobedient female is thrust into cultural centrality as a lightning rod to absorb and contain the society's amorphously circulating anxieties about the interlocked issues of dominance and subordination.

Inside *The Shrew*'s narrative model of male success, Kate's ultimate function is to make Petruchio a winner, which status he achieves through the wager he makes on his wife's proficiency in subjection. And, by the terms of his bet—"Twenty crowns! / I'll venture so much of my hawk or hound, / But twenty times so much upon my wife," Petruchio acquires the preemptive privilege of a narrative entrance into the emparkment of superior status previously owned by the aristocratic Lord, who had entered the stage likewise venturing a bet beyond twenty pounds on his well-trained prize bitch.

Male Dream of Success

For a theater audience, it is Petruchio who carries the middle- and lower-class male viewer's fused fantasies of erotic reward, financial success, and upward social mobility.

What we know from the terms of the play is that, although Petruchio seems to have inherited a respectable amount of land, to guarantee an apparently otherwise precarious hold on upward mobility he has by necessity embarked on an openly acknowledged quest to wive it wealthily and, if wealthily, then well. As Gremio tells us, his master is flat broke and would marry an old trot if she had money enough. And although Hortensio can afford to insist that he would not marry a shrew for a mine of gold, Petruchio's financial exigencies make him assert, "thou know'st not gold's effect." In the play's subliminal class structure, everything we know about Petruchio's situation suggests that he is in the predicament of a land-poor son whose father acquired enough land to stake a claim on the future, but who, like many others trying during this era to defend their newly won status, urgently needs ready cash to protect his gains against the various new fines, taxes, costs of enclosing, and other assessments that powerful and land-hungry owners kept successfully pushing into county legislation to force their less solvent neighbors to sell. In wiving it wealthily, Petruchio manages to prove himself not only a good husband to his patrimonial inheritance but a better son-in-law than even Lucentio, the rich young Pisan whose class background announces itself in various ways throughout his opening speech of act I including the information he there provides about his father, "A merchant of great traffic through the world, / Vincentio, come of the Bentivolii; / Vincentio's son, brought up in Florence."

PETRUCHIO'S UPWARD MOBILITY RESEMBLES SHAKESPEARE'S

In this play, the fantasy of a bourgeois (male) culture achieves a fully satisfying statement: upward mobility, displacement of one's supposed betters through the entrepreneurial success of deeds, and a new hierarchy of male relations no longer strictly defined by social class as birthright. The story is, essentially, a paradigm of the success story of the English yeomanry. And the fact of Petruchio's location in that class origin is strongly suggested through the connection the Induction sets up between Petruchio and the actor whom the Lord apparently singles out to play him—the actor whom the Lord praises for his verisimilitude in playing "a farmer's eldest son" in a play "where you wooed the gentlewoman so well" that the "part / Was aptly fitted and naturally perform'd." The yeomanry was likewise the status group that defined Shakespeare's own origins and was the social class within which at least some—including both John and William Shakespeare—made significant gains during the shift to agrarian capitalism. But furthermore, it was the class that in the early 1590s seems already to have evolved into something of a universal signifier, as capable as is the status of "middle class" in present-day America of carrying the projections of even the Slys of the world, as unmaterializable as their desires might ultimately prove to be. . . .

Within the fiction that Petruchio enacts, "deeds" are in every way preeminent. It is a new world of opportunity and opportunism, one in which Sly's claim to being a "lord indeed" translates into Petruchio's entitlement to being a lord in deeds. For Petruchio is, as he several times says, the man who "would fain be doing." And yet, as the dowry negotiations that so repeatedly enter into this play attest, "deeds" is never wholly separate from a reference to land titles.

Battle of the Social Classes

Even the famous Kate and Petruchio battle of wills is waged through the vocabulary of class, most of which for an audience today no longer carry the same weight. At the moment Signior Baptista's elder daughter enters the stage, Petruchio greets her with an instant demotion from the aristocratic "Katherine" by which she defines herself to the distinctly common "Kate"—and "plain Kate, / And bonny Kate, and sometimes Kate the curst." In her suggestion to Petruchio to "Remove you hence. I knew you at the first / You were a movable" lies the disdaining insult by which Kate identifies her suitor as one of England's newly mobile social groups, either a vagabond or a social climber attempting to move up. In saying she is "too light for such a swain as you to catch," she mocks his courtship as that of a country bumpkin. The tenor of most of the courtship consists, in fact, of a series of loaded class insults in which Kate repeatedly hits at the evident inferiority of Petruchio's status while Petruchio parries by repeatedly bringing Kate down to level terms and treating her more like a barnyard wench than a gentlewoman:

> PET.   What, with my tongue in your tail? Nay, come again.
> Good Kath, I am a gentleman—
> KATH.   That I'll try.   [*She strikes him.*]
> PET.   I swear I'll cuff you if you strike again.

KATH. So may you lose your arms.
      If you strike me, you are no gentleman,
      And if no gentleman, why then no arms.
PET.   A herald, Kate? O put me in thy books!
KATH. What is your crest—a coxcomb?

Likewise, Kate's complaint to her father

Call you me "daughter"? . . .
You have show'd a tender fatherly regard,
To wish me wed to one half-lunatic,
A madcap ruffian and a swearing Jack,
That thinks with oaths to face the matter out

is likewise grounded in terms that protest the class basis of
the proposed match. And although Signior Baptista—happy
that anyone will marry Kate—never mentions such a class
differential, it seems obvious enough to the rich old nobleman Gremio, whose caustic observations about Petruchio
and comments to him throughout the play reveal a distinct
class disdain. On the wedding day, when Petruchio arrives
dressed as a vagabond in order to humiliate Kate and bring
her to par, it is Signior Gremio, for instance, who comments,
"A bridegroom, say you? 'tis a groom indeed, / A grumbling
groom, and that the girl shall find."

KATE LOSES CLASS STATUS BY MARRYING

But it is the term "gentle" and Petruchio's ability to manipu-
late it that defines the ultimate weapon in the play's arsenal
of class threats and insults because slippage in this term was
propelling it into an insidious link between the discourses of
gender and class. When Petruchio says to Kate, "I find you
passing gentle," his reference is to a term of gender, not
class. When he denies her the cap that all the "gentlewomen
wear" by saying, "When you are gentle you shall have one
too, / And not till then," he again switches the reference from
her assumption of entitlement based on class status to one
that makes it contingent on the exhibition of appropriately
submissive female behavior, a standard of gender defined by
male authority. And though it is most likely true, as Kate an-
grily exclaims, that "your betters have endur'd me say my
mind," Petruchio has by marriage acquired the power to ma-
nipulate the signifiers that define Kate's social status and de-
termine just who her "betters" will be. . . .

The class privileges that Kate acquired through birth are
now, ironically enough, privileges to which she has access
only through her husband. Like the signifying cap and gown

that Petruchio dangles in front of her only to whisk away, retention of her class status is a privilege that he has made contingent on her conceding male supremacy. . . .

Within this emerging vision, Kate's rebellious demand for self-sovereignty falls prey to the substitute pleasures of a highly gendered, patriarchally overlaid model of social class in which femaleness is conceived as a privileged object made to decorate male life. . . .

Feminine achievement is conceived as making it successfully into wifehood, and therein becoming the pampered object of a dedicated provider who, "for thy maintenance; commits his body / To painful labour. . . . Whilst thou liest warm at home, secure and safe." Gone is the Katherina whom Hortensio described as like to prove herself a soldier after she had quite literally broken the lute on him; gone is the Kate who struck Petruchio and threatened to comb old Gremio's noddle with a three-legged stool. In its place in Kate's concluding vision is the model of physical helplessness that will shortly become the romantic axiom for the eroticized feminine object. The speech thus marks a clear historical point at which womanhood has been reconceived into the erotic fantasy of exquisitely helpless fragility, of having a body that is "soft, and weak, and smooth, / Unapt to toil and trouble in the world"; a body whose "soft condition," being endowed with only "strength as weak, [and] weakness past compare.". . .

The vision of true womanhood that Kate presents us with is, finally, the fantasy of being a gentle/woman—a putatively helpless object of leisure, enclosed and immured in masculine protection, born to shop and displayed forth in the fashionable signs of aristocratic status which Petruchio makes Kate realize he can and will withhold from her. Unless Kate becomes a gentle woman, she will remain in the low status of having to beg the servants for food, in every way infantilized, deprived of all authority, indefinitely dressed in "honest, mean habiliments," and thus signified with all the low-status cultural capital that announces her position in the world as perilously close to that of the beggar who watches this play. . . .

Within the vision that Kate is constructed to dramatize, the trade-offs for which she settles exchange desire for equality in one hierarchy for the guaranteed material and social privileges of another. . . .

KATE SUBMITS—DISEMPOWERMENT *IS* HISTORICAL

In this play, as is frequently true in gender and class relations in general, beneath every asserted dominance is inevitably an unacknowledged, uncredited, and usually unpaid dependency of the higher on the lower. Like Sly, Petruchio moves from his initial status as a needy wanderer to the bed of a highborn wife; and, like Sly, Petruchio depends for his lordship on the signifying speech act of a madam wife who, positioned as she is within the gender hierarchy, is the one person who can make lord and husband interchangeable terms. Sly's first anxious demand of his madam wife is that she call him husband. And obediently: "My husband and my lord, my lord and husband, / I am your wife in all obedience," intones Sly's wife. In her words, the play anticipates the parallel lines through which Petruchio's wife will elevate him into metaphoric peerage and women in the audience will be enjoined likewise to elevate their husbands: "Thy husband is thy lord, thy life, thy keeper, / Thy head, thy sovereign," says Kate. But Sly's madam wife has always been, of course, little Bartholomew, the Lord's page, who has been commanded by the Lord to dress up like a lady and serve the Lord's voyeuristic desires by playing out a wifely acquiescence that will convince the hapless Sly that he, too, is a lord indeed. . . . To Sly's query whether the Kate and Petruchio play at hand is a "comonty," a "Christmas gambold," a "tumbling-trick," or some "household stuff" Bartholomew—speaking right at the juncture between frame and inner play, right between the Warwickshire ground and its Padua displacement—solemnly rejects all these farcical categories. Instead, he insists: "No, my good lord, it is more pleasing stuff. . . . / It is a kind of history." And so, perhaps, it is.

CHAPTER 2

Themes and Ideas Developed in *The Taming of the Shrew*

The Taming of the Shrew Mocks the World of Mercantile Marriage

Gareth Lloyd Evans

Gareth Lloyd Evans is a lecturer in dramatic literature at Birmington University, England, and a theater
critic of international reputation. In this selection
from his book *The Upstart Crow*, Lloyd Evans identifies two opposing attitudes about marriage during the
Elizabethan period: marriage as a true union of
hearts and minds, and marriage as a business
arrangement. Though the mercantile world of profit
and loss, commodities and stocks, permeates the
play, Lloyd Evans argues that Petruchio and Kate
achieve a true union of heart and mind by defying
the values of the mercantile world; nevertheless, to
prove their achievement to the world they have tran-
scended, they must demonstrate success on its terms.

[The] world [in the *Taming of the Shrew*] . . . is mercantile to
the end; bargaining is its element, and, even at the conclusion of its biggest transaction (the marriage of Bianca), the
gambling element remains in the final wager. We see it in
action in Act II when Gremio, Baptista and Tranio argue
about who has most to give as a dowry. Even the slightly
more romantic Hortensio expresses his feelings for Bianca
in material terms. She is, to him, a 'treasure', 'a jewel' and he
consoles his disappointment with a rich widow. Because of
the comic spirit which hangs about this world, it seems less
sour and mean than limited in intelligence and emotional
responses. For this reason Bianca herself, the prize in the
lottery, is less attractive than her fiery sister, for Bianca belongs to this world of commodity and in all probability her
whole future married life will be based on the stocks and
shares of wedlock, not on the realities of true love.

KATE REJECTS A MATERIALIST WORLD

Significantly, Kate does not seem a part of all this. It is not just that she is set apart because of her temper, but because of her implied attitude to this materialistic world—in itself a cause of her impatience. Even in her wilder moments she has a more refined conception of love. When she physically attacks and berates Bianca, it is not mere shrewishness, but a desire for truth that emerges:

'Of all thy suitors here I charge thee tell
Whom thou lov'st best. See thou dissemble not.'

When she gets an equivocal answer, she says:

'O then, belike, you fancy riches more.'

She is set apart from this profit and loss world, not just because she is less marketable than Bianca but because she rejects it, by losing her temper with its ways. She is, as it were,

---

MARRIAGE AND MONEY

In this selection from The Bedford Companion to Shakespeare, *Russ McDonald explains sixteenth-century matrimonial customs and priorities.*

In the words of a sixteenth-century proverb, "More belongs to marriage than four bare legs in a bed." Marriage was part of a system of inheritance and economics so ingrained and pervasive that the emotional affections or physical desires of a man and woman diminished in importance. This was especially true among the upper classes, where the amount of property being inherited could be substantial, and where marriage was regarded as a convenient instrument for joining or ensuring peace between two powerful families, for consolidating land holdings, or for achieving other familial, financial, or even political ends. Once a marriage was agreed on, certain fiscal transactions took place. The bride's family promised to give to the married couple a *dowry* made up of property, valuables (silver and jewelry, for example), and cash. This was also called the bride's *portion,* and it was paid at the time of the wedding or soon after, occasionally in installments. If a young man could find a young woman whose family could afford a substantial dowry, then he could look forward to living comfortably. Moreover, his parents might be able to save some of their holdings to settle on their other children, perhaps their own daughters. The groom's family agreed to provide the couple with money to live on, to specify exactly what the

in a limbo—not having found a world with values which
will enable it to love her for what she is.

PETRUCHIO APPEARS ONLY MERCENARY

At first, the auguries are bad. Petruchio seems even more
mercantile than the rest—'Why, nothing comes amiss so
money come withal'. He is bland about his intentions:

'I come to wive it wealthily in Padua;
If wealthily, then happily in Padua.'

Indeed Shakespeare so emphasizes this aspect of Petruchio
(he is even more efficient at bargaining than the rest) that
one's suspicions are aroused that a deep purpose lies behind. Its nature is not long delayed. As soon as he meets
Kate his references to the mercantile aspects of marriage
have a different tone. When he speaks now of 'bargain' it is

groom would inherit at his father's death, and to guarantee a
dower (the parallel term to dowry), the sum that the bride
would inherit should the groom die before her. This money,
also called the *jointure*, served as a kind of life insurance for
the bride. In fact, it is useful to think of all of these settlements
as a form of security, both for the couple being married and
for the families sending them out into the world. The mone-
tary arrangements I have described were designed to guarantee that the couple would live comfortably, and that if one
partner should die the other would not be penniless or a drain
on his or her family.

The complexities and permutations of this system were considerable, of course, but a few generalizations can be made
about sixteenth- and seventeenth-century practices. It was better to have sons than daughters. Because primogeniture en-
sured that an estate was passed on intact from father to eldest
son, that young man's prospects were very bright. His parents
sought the daughter of a prominent or wealthy family whose
dowry would be worthy of the inheritance he would receive. If
his parents were dead, he presented himself to the family of an
appropriate partner, as Petruchio does in *The Taming of the
Shrew*. Indeed, consciousness of these economic and social customs makes such Shakespearean suitors as Petruchio and Clau-
dio in *Much Ado About Nothing* look less like fortune hunters
and more like prudent conservators of their familial legacy.

Russ McDonald, ed., *The Bedford Companion to Shakespeare.* New York: Bedford
Books of St. Martin's Press, 1996.

to a secret one between her and him—alone. When he arrives, tattered, at the wedding, he shouts—'to me she's married not unto my clothes'. Most significantly, before he bears her away he returns to commodity, but the tone is mocking and dismissive:

> 'She is my goods, my chattels, she is my house,
> My household stuff, my field, my barn,
> My horse, my ox, my ass, my any thing,
> And here she stands; touch her whoever dare;'

but he adds—'fear not, sweet wench, they shall not touch thee, Kate.' Love makes him mock what is merely material. In his determination to win Kate the means he uses amount to a denial of the values of commodity. He deprives her and himself in order to win her from any lingering affiliations with the trappings of the other world. When they are stripped away, nothing is left—save love:

> 'And where two raging fires meet together,
> They do consume the thing that feeds their fury.'

Kate resists, partly because she believes she has been traded to this man—and at a knock-down price. She is shrewish for this reason, certainly, but also because she cannot believe that this one is any different from others. Her experience on her wedding night begins to convince her that he is, and she too begins to change, as they both begin to move into their own mutually acceptable world. Shakespeare emphasizes the difference between their world and the one they have left, through the great comic scene which precedes their arrival at Petruchio's house. Petruchio has his plans laid, but it is a desperate lot he casts. . . . We are given the account of the journey home—no romantic idyll but a slogging match in the mud. Grumio ends his account, in its way as trenchant as the account of Gadshill, with the words:

> '. . . winter tames man, woman, and beast; for it hath tam'd my old master, and my new mistress, and myself, fellow Curtis.'

The scene with the tailor equally fulfils a double role. It is fine, broad, visual comedy but it suggests more—it represents the final committal of both of them, after a hard fight, to naked love as opposed to mere partnership:

> 'For 'tis the mind that makes the body rich;'

The scene of their return journey is as important in emphasizing the change that has occurred in Kate as the wedding scene is in what it tells us about Petruchio. She has, by now, been 'tamed', and the 'taming' involves a recognition that the reality of love is more important than outward word or show. In their new-found but still cautious delight in one another they play a game which is a smiling impersonation of the old confusion they had both made between illusion and reality. They can now afford, in delighted consort, to make it a game, because neither is any longer alone—they have found their world. On its comic level this scene is one of the most affirmative of love's truth in the whole of the early plays.

KATE AND PETRUCHIO CONQUER THE MERCANTILE WORLD

Yet one thing remains to do—they have to conquer the world of commodity which they left. They return to prove to us, and to Padua, the truth of their metamorphosis, achieving that proof in the terms of that mercantile world—by a wager, so making its validity all the more relevant for having made use of the rules of that world. Kate's last speech puts the case for the natural correctness of woman's submitting to man. This would have been understood and applauded by the Elizabethans. Yet if any other wife in the play had made this speech it would have been a mere formality. We know, Kate knows, Petruchio knows, and Shakespeare knows that, behind the formal words, there is a deeper meaning. Kate and her husband have won each other by love, and within its total truth such things as honour, obey, and submit, are not bits and snaffles but wings. It is a celebration of the mystery of love's wealth—where 'property was thus appalled' and 'Either was the other's mine'.

The Themes of Education and Metamorphosis Unify the Play

Brian Morris

Brian Morris offers a perceptive analysis of two related themes in *The Taming of the Shrew:* education
and metamorphosis. Both education and metamorphosis involve change. While education advances intellectual and moral change, metamorphosis suggests a broader range of changes, from alteration of
appearance to complete transformation of character.

In his introduction to the Arden edition of Shakespeare's
plays, Morris explains Elizabethan educational practices,
then analyzes the multiple references to education in *The
Taming of the Shrew*. The play, Morris argues, contrasts
formal education with Petruchio's unorthodox approach,
and it clearly demonstrates the effectiveness of Petruchio's
teaching methods. His pupil, Kate, grows and changes; she
learns appropriate social behavior and experiences intellectual liberation.

Multiple allusions to Ovid's *Metamorphoses* suggest the
play's overall emphasis on change. Superficial changes are
indicated by changes in clothing. Sly is dressed as a lord;
Barthol'mew the page is dressed as a wife; Lucentio and
Hortensio dress as tutors; servants dress as masters. In
each case the transformations are temporary and easily re-
versed. By contrast, Kate experiences a change in character.
She is transformed from a shrew to a "pleasant, gamesome,
passing courteous" woman. Her transformation is substantial and permanent.

All formal education is, in some sense, a reduction to conformity, a restraint upon freedom. The child is subjected to

Excerpted from *Taming of the Shrew,* edited by Brian Morris. *The Arden Edition of the
Works of William Shakespeare* (London: Methuen). Copyright ©1981 Methuen & Co.
Ltd. (editorial matter). Reprinted by permission of Thomas Nelson and Sons Ltd.

experiences not of its own choosing, introduced to preferred patterns of social behaviour, expected to comply. Before anything can be drawn out of the individual mind, much is put in, and the line between liberal education and socio-cultural indoctrination is difficult to draw and harder to hold. Elizabethan educationists were less concerned with liberating the pupil's consciousness by encouragement to free-ranging enquiry than with inculcating an approved body of knowledge in the context of a serenely accepted social order, to the end that the young might grow up literate, useful citizens of the commonwealth, and, if possible, good and wise as well. *The Shrew* both illustrates this and explores its limitations. But the accepted background must be borne in mind.

The Induction offers the theme obliquely. In his 'practice' upon Sly the Lord conducts an experiment in human nature, so that Sly is offered a picture of himself as a cultured English gentleman—hunting, hawking, but also taking delight in music, pictures, and the performance of plays. Sly, however, remains resolutely himself, rural, vulgar and illiterate, although vastly attracted by the pleasures of gentility, illustrating the truth that education cannot be imposed, it must be achieved. Sly belongs with Barnadine and Caliban in Shakespeare's gallery of the incorrigible and ineducable, upon whose natures nurture can never stick. The opening of the main play sets up a strong contrast. Lucentio comes to Padua to institute 'A course of learning and ingenious studies' and seeking the 'happiness / By virtue specially to be achiev'd'. Padua was famous throughout Europe as a university city, the centre of Aristotelianism, and a debate ensues between Lucentio and Tranio about the curriculum to be followed. Tranio advocates a wide syllabus, philosophy, logic, rhetoric, music, poetry and mathematics, balancing the discipline of Aristotle against sweet witty Ovid on the doubtful principle that 'no profit grows where is no pleasure ta'en', and ends with the permissive prescription 'study what you most affect'. We feel that this intellectual voyage 'is but for two months victuall'd'. The entry of Bianca with her family puts an end to this academic planning and we never hear of it again. But the brisk bargaining and match-making which follows in I.i creates a contrast between the world of romantic love, allied to cultural and intellectual pursuits, and the world of realistic marriage contracts, made in a society of merchants and adventurers.

Education has a high social value in Padua, as we see from the stately conduct of the episode (in ii.i) in which the disguised suitors are presented to Baptista as tutors. Both are described as 'cunning' men, and he is careful to instruct that they should be 'used well'. Yet the formal lessons we hear of or witness are parodies of instruction. Hortensio's impatient pupil breaks his lute over his head, and when he and Lucentio wrangle over who shall instruct Bianca first (iii.i), the pupil seizes the opportunity to assume the master's role. Lucentio makes his Latin lesson a cover for declaring his love, and Hortensio puts his music to the same use. The effect of all this is to depreciate the value of booklearning, or, at least, to show that artistic and intellectual pursuits have little attraction against the pull of 'love, first learned in a lady's eyes'. This is precisely the demonstration Shakespeare makes in his most intellectual and erudite comedy, *Love's Labour's Lost.* It is epitomized in *The Shrew* at the opening of iv.ii, where Tranio and Hortensio overhear the brief love-conversation between Lucentio and Bianca:

> LUC. Now, mistress, profit you in what you read?
> BIAN. What, master, read you? First resolve me that.
> LUC. I read that I profess, *The Art to Love.*
> BIAN. And may you prove, sir, master of your art.

The point is that Ovid's *Ars Amatoria* is anything but a manual for romantic lovers. It is a witty, cynical textbook for seducers, offering here an ironic comment on Lucentio's wooing methods and Bianca's mixture of naïveté, sentiment and calculation.

PETRUCHIO'S UNORTHODOX TEACHING METHODS

The play makes clear that the true paths to learning are not those of the school or university. Formal education is contrasted to its detriment against the practical academy of experience. Here, as elsewhere, Petruchio stands at the centre of the stage. He is the teacher, Katherina is his pupil. His task is to inculcate such knowledge and instil such behaviour as will fit her to take a useful place in the existing society. The play gives his qualifications, and is significantly concerned to demonstrate his teaching methods in an exemplary way. His first appearance, in i.ii, shows him ready to use his fists to teach Grumio how to knock at a door when he is told; this teacher is direct, practical, distinctly rough and very ready, and intent on being master. When presented with the prospect of educating Katherina into conformity he presents his credentials:

> Have I not in my time heard lions roar?
> Have I not heard the sea, puff'd up with winds,
> Rage like an angry boar chafed with sweat?
> Have I not heard great ordnance in the field,
> And heaven's artillery thunder in the skies?
> Have I not in a pitched battle heard
> Loud 'larums, neighing steeds, and trumpets' clang?
> And do you tell me of a woman's tongue,
> That gives not half so great a blow to hear
> As will a chestnut in a farmer's fire?
> Tush, tush, fear boys with bugs!

He has faced many things, and his experience gives him confidence that he is a strong candidate for this post.

His teaching technique is a rich and strange mixture of the academic and the practical. At the heart of it lies the most commendable pedagogic principle of presenting his pupil with an image of what he wants her to become:

> Take this of me, Kate of my consolation,
> Hearing thy mildness prais'd in every town,
> Thy virtues spoke of, and thy beauty sounded,
> Yet not so deeply as to thee belongs,
> Myself am mov'd to woo thee for my wife.

Throughout the play this ideal picture is constantly kept before Katherina, and she is gradually wooed and induced into conformity with it. Part of Petruchio's technique is coercive: he gives as good as he gets in the flyting [verbal duel] match of ii.i, he subjects his pupil to disgrace and humiliation in the wedding scene, and he deliberately keeps her without food or sleep in the testing scenes of Act iv. But it is significant that he never physically assaults or chastises her, and this sharply distinguishes *The Shrew* from earlier plays on the taming theme like *Tom Tyler and his Wife*. The larger part of Petruchio's teaching method is puzzlement. Katherina is reluctantly fascinated by his energetic and outrageous behaviour (there is no precedent for it in the Padua of her upbringing), and she only gradually comes to recognize it as a travesty of her own wild behaviour. The audience, duly instructed by Petruchio's two explicit soliloquies, can watch the series of lessons from a position of informed superiority. Katherina has to work out, incident by incident, the significance of the instruction she is being given. All this is so unlike the normal processes of Elizabethan education, with its rote learning of grammar and syntax, its translation and retranslation, its imitation of approved literary and philosophical models, that it hardly looks like a teaching process at all. But the subject, the bringing to conformity of an aberrant member of a social group, was no part of any school curriculum, though it was the first premise and ultimate object of all schooling. Petruchio's teaching task, self-imposed, is to bring Katherina into conformity with the acceptable social image of a marriageable young woman in 'Paduan' society. . . . The unorthodoxy, and novelty, of this educational programme is the central point of interest in the play's exploration of teaching and learning, and all the other lessons are subservient and contributory to it.

Katherina, however, is not Petruchio's only pupil, and he varies his methods according to his students. Grumio, in I.ii, is taught by the most direct method, a box on the ear. Hortensio and Lucentio, the pupil-teachers, are given the example of the 'taming school', and exhorted to follow it. These are the traditional and time-honoured techniques; Petruchio's innovation in educational methodology lies in his treatment of Katherina. It is still capable of raising heated debate when the play is performed on the stage, and perhaps this is because it presents with alarming directness the dichotomy which underlies all educative processes. On the one hand, education is designed to liberate and bring to full fruition the innate capabilities of the pupil. On the other, it is a means of reducing the individual to social conformity through the imparting of approved knowledge and acceptable skills. To some extent it is always a taming procedure, at odds with the very human desire for liberty. But it also works on the deep human need to conform and to be socially approved within the tribe. The tension between these contrary impulses is always present. *The Taming of the Shrew* makes them uncomfortably evident.

METAMORPHOSIS

Education is one way of transforming a person into someone else, but it is not the only form of change the play investigates. The theme of transformation, of metamorphosis, raises perhaps some of the subtlest questions in the play but it does so through the medium of very direct allusion and reference, and in some of the play's most obvious stage action. It is notable that most of the reference to classical mythology takes place in the early part of the play, where it serves a variety of purposes. . . .

At the very opening we are presented with the spectacle of a man transformed into a beast. The Lord, approaching the sleeping Sly, comments: 'O monstrous beast, how like a swine he lies.' He at once resolves to 'practise on this drunken man' and transform him into a lord, asking his huntsmen: 'Would not the beggar then forget himself?' Such transformations, up and down the social scale, with the participants either losing their old identities or shrewdly retaining them, are to become essential ingredients of the play's action. No sooner has the transformation of Sly been agreed than the actors enter, themselves professional shape-shifters, and they are enlisted to take part in the sport 'Wherein your cunning can assist me much'. The scene ends with instructions sent to 'Barthol'mew my page' to transform himself into a lady and play the drunkard's wife. In the second scene of the Induction Sly stubbornly resists the possibility that he has been metamorphosed into a lord, until he is seduced by the images of Cytherea, Io and Daphne, all taken directly from Ovid's *Metamorphoses,* into exclaiming: 'Upon my life, I am a lord indeed.' The comic significance of what he then says and does in performance of his new role lies, of course, in his inability to play the part. His metamorphosis must be imperfect because he is ignorant of how to behave. But the whole game of shape-changing in the Induction is proleptic [anticipates] of the metamorphoses in the main play. One character after another assumes a disguise, practises to deceive, and takes on a new identity. . . . The disguised Page of the Induction prefigures the obedient and compliant wife which Katherina becomes in v.ii. The bewildered Sly, incapable through ignorance of changing himself, contrasts with the Katherina who slowly and painstakingly learns her part.

As the main play opens, Lucentio hopes, by the study of Aristotelian virtue, to transform himself into a scholar, but Tranio reminds him that this might be a barren role if 'Ovid be an outcast quite abjured', which links the poet of the *Metamorphoses* with that of the *Amores*, which is to be the lovers' textbook. The first sight of Bianca transforms Lucentio instantly into a lover, and he likens her beauty to that of 'the daughter of Agenor'. According to Ovid (*Metamorphoses,* ii. 846–75) Agenor's daughter, Europa, was the beloved of

Jupiter, who appeared before her transformed into a snow-white bull. And so the transformation game goes on, through allusion and action. The love-plot brings about the exchange of clothing and identity between Lucentio and Tranio (the first of the 'disguisings' in the play), and Tranio *becomes* his master for most of the rest of the action. In II.i Lucentio becomes Cambio, and Hortensio becomes Litio, so that, through the central Acts of the play, nearly half the cast are not what they seem. These metamorphoses are relatively simple, parts of the machinery of the plot, and true identities can be resumed by so simple a device as the changing of clothes. Like the Pedant, and Vincentio, later, they are all, as Biondello says, 'busied about a counterfeit assurance', and no one of them is ever in doubt about his true identity.

KATE'S TRANSFORMATION

Sly, however, is unsure of himself. If, as I believe, the play originally contained Induction, episodes and Epilogue, it seems clear that he was intended to remain bewildered. Reluctantly, and because it seemed the best thing to do, he assumes the identity of the Lord, and at the end of the play he equally reluctantly becomes a beggar again. He is perpetually bewildered, and in this he is the prefiguration of Katherina, who, once Petruchio accosts her, is never allowed to be sure of her own nature until she surrenders to the character he has created for her. She is secure, if discontented, as the typical 'shrew' in II.i, and this is the identity she offers to Petruchio in the flyting match. But, in spite of the evidence, he refuses to believe her, assuming that she is 'pleasant, gamesome, passing courteous, . . . sweet as spring-time flowers'. This is the dislocating picture, held up to her as a mirror to nature for the rest of the play. And the mutation of her personality which takes place is achieved not with the ease of a change of clothes, but with difficulty, with reluctance, with recalcitrance. Yet the metamorphosis is permanent. Just as the changes in Ovid's *Metamorphoses* are mutations which preserve the life of the subject, or apotheosize [glorify] his or her state, so the change in Katherina is shown as a development into a better, and enduring, condition. And, in keeping with the bewildering changes in which the play abounds, Petruchio brings her change about by himself assuming a variety of roles. The bluff, rough wooer of Act II is succeeded in III.ii by the fantastic bridegroom, coming to his wedding 'in a pair of old breeches thrice turned'. The purpose of this disguise is to enforce upon Katherina her own unpreparedness for marriage, just as the roistering bully Petruchio becomes in iv.i and iv.iii is a means of displaying to his wife her own inability to manage a household and command her servants. As Peter says, 'He kills her in her own humour'.

Although the majority of references to Ovid occur in the earlier scenes of the play, the poet maintains a presence as late as Act iv. In iii.i Lucentio invites Bianca to construe a passage from the *Heroides*, and in iv.ii he instructs her in the *Ars Amatoria*. It is as if the mythological Ovid of the *Metamorphoses* gives place, as the play progresses, to the sweet, witty poet of love. The play's development is in tune with this, for the dazzling changes of identity in the manifold disguisings take place, for the most part, in the first two Acts, while the later part of the play is concerned with the longer rhythms of the change of personality which overcomes Katherina. It is upon her transformation that we focus, though we may note the foil which Shakespeare provides for her in her sister. Bianca is the only major character who assumes no disguise, and achieves no development. She begins, in i.i, with her own form of covert and clever shrewishness to her sister, securing herself the sympathy of her father and all his household, and she ends the play bidding fair to take up where her sister left off. The morality of *The Shrew* is a morality of change.

The Transforming Power of Plays and Play-Acting

Alvin B. Kernan

Most people play several roles; some of these roles are imposed on us by figures of authority or by our own sense of duty, while others allow us to express our mood or to evoke responses from others. As a man of the theater and a student of human nature, Shakespeare was vitally interested in the effect of acting or role-playing on the individual and on the audience watching the individual (or watching a professional play).

Former Yale English professor and Princeton humanities professor Alvin B. Kernan focuses on these two recurring concerns: the effect of acting or role-playing on individuals, and the effect of theatrical performances on the audience. "All the world *is* a stage in Padua, where the theater is the only true image of life," Kernan says. In this selection from his book *The Playwright as Magician*, Kernan explores the different reasons for the characters' role-playing in *The Taming of the Shrew*.

The Taming of the Shrew is a theatrical tour de force in the use of the play-within-the-play, consisting of plays set within plays and actors watching other actors acting, seemingly extending into infinity. All the world is a stage in Padua, where the theater is the only true image of life. In the outermost frame-play a drunken tinker, Christopher Sly, is picked out of the mud by a rich lord and transported to his house. A little pretense is arranged, purely for amusement, and when Sly awakes he finds himself in rich surroundings, addressed as a nobleman, obeyed in every wish, and waited on by a beautiful wife.

REASONS FOR ROLE-PLAYING

At this point a group of professional traveling players appears to the sound of trumpets to provide entertainment in the great house. They are warmly welcomed and fed, and are asked to put on a play for the tinker, who is represented as a noble and eccentric lord. The inner play about the taming of the shrew, which the players then perform, is in turn filled with many other instances of playing. Young men disguise themselves in order to marry beautiful young girls and get their fathers' money, while servants play masters and masters play servants, all for pleasure and profit, in the most literal sense of those famous Horatian terms. Petruchio arrives "to wive it wealthily in Padua" and finds that theatrical methods alone will enable him to transform the beautiful and wealthy Kate from a cursed shrew, useless to herself and anyone else, into a loving and happy wife. Wooing as playing begins at once as Petruchio pretends that Kate is in all ways the very opposite of what in fact she is:

> Say that she rail, why then I'll tell her plain
> She sings as sweetly as a nightingale.
> Say that she frown, I'll say she looks as clear
> As morning roses newly washed with dew.

His acting intrigues Kate, at least to the extent that she agrees to marry him.

Petruchio's greatest play is staged on his wedding day when he appears in a fantastic, ragged costume and takes Kate on a wild ride through the rain and cold to an isolated country house where he forces her to fast, to remain awake and to endure a number of frustrations to her will, all the time pretending that he is concerned only for her well being. Playing is here an instrument of power which enables Petruchio to dominate Kate, force her to play in his play, but it also shows Kate "feelingly" the misery of a household and human relationships in which one selfish will is set absolutely against all others. She gives no indication of having consciously learned the moral lesson that the play's mirror holds up to her, but in order to protect herself and procure the necessary food, clothing, rest, and return to life within the social community, represented by the return from the isolated country house to Padua and her father's home, she herself learns to become a player.

However, the playing has had its effect, even though, as is

so often the case in Shakespeare, the "audience" responds with only rudimentary surface understanding of what they have seen and been moved by. Kate has been changed by Petruchio's pretense, even if she does not understand, or at least does not speak of, its full meaning and power, and at the end of the play we see a Kate who can cheerfully say that the sun is the moon or can pretend to be absolutely subservient to a husband's will if domestic tranquility so requires. She has perhaps not been broken to her husband's will, nor even, perhaps, become more sweet-tempered, if generations of actors have interpreted the play properly, but she has at least learned that living and loving both require considerable pretense.

RESULTS OF ROLE-PLAYING

Like opposed mirrors, the inner play of the Shrew and the outer play of Christopher Sly reveal the same truth by reverse means. In both cases some disordered and wasted portion of humanity has been transformed and redeemed by means of a play and acting, but Sly is shown what he might find in a positive sense—a noble life—Kate in a negative—a life of misery and deprivation. In both cases the desired end can be achieved only by play-acting. Kate acts out her understanding dramatically by pretending to obey absolutely and to believe everything Petruchio says, while Sly acknowledges the wonderful powers of art by proclaiming that he is no longer one of those ancient Slys who "came in with Richard Conqueror," but has become something new and wonderful:

> Am I a lord, and have I such a lady?
> Or do I dream? Or have I dreamed till now?
> I do not sleep: I see, I hear, I speak,
> I smell sweet savors and I feel soft things.
> Upon my life, I am a lord indeed
> And not a tinker nor Christopher Sly.

The Shrew dramatizes the traditional Horatian view that the function of comedy is both to please and to instruct, achieving these ends not by directly imitating reality, but by creating exaggerated and distorted images of life which show Sly how wonderful the world could be and show Kate how terrible it could become. The play, however, expands the modest claim of pleasure and profit to suggest that the histrionic art not only instructs in a right and pleasurable way of life but is also itself literally the means of reaching happiness and pleasure, in the theater and in life. Restage the world and the life within it can be utterly changed! Art can make drunken tinkers and savage shrews into noble lords and loving spouses.

THEATER'S TRANSFORMING POWER

The claims for the power of the theater are large and confident in *The Shrew*, but at the same time the play glances uneasily at the real circumstances of the Elizabethan theatrical world in which plays had to try to realize their near-magical powers of transformation. The motives for theatrical performance are no higher than a simple desire for amusement by the nobleman who picks Sly out of the gutter, and the crudest kind of desire for economic profit in the case of Petruchio and the other internal actors. And despite the miraculous transformations achieved by playing, art works its magic without either the actors or the stage audiences fully understanding what happens to them. The chief actor, Petruchio, exults crudely and openly in the wealth he has won and his absolute power over his "audience" wife, while Kate, Sly, and others, the first of Shakespeare's many uncomprehending audiences, are changed radically by their encounter with theater, but without quite knowing what has taken place. . . .

The Shrew reveals Shakespeare's characteristic stance throughout his career as a playwright in the theater. Theater is an art form, not mere entertainment, and a play proves its right to the status of art by its ability to show men, even if for only an instant, what they and their world might ideally become, and even provides them with a model of how the transformation might actually be wrought. But at the same time, the actual conditions of theatrical production are not as ideal as might be desired, and the doubtful motives and limited comprehension of actors and audiences represent not only the situation the playwright had to deal with in presenting his play in the theater, but the stubborn, intractable nature of reality itself which his illusion had to try to overcome.

The Shrew is, however, on the whole optimistic about the powers of theatrical art.

The Stage Power of the Female Heroine

Juliet Dusinberre

Most twentieth-century students of Shakespeare know that boy actors played the female roles on the Renaissance stage, but few consider the implications of this practice. Juliet Dusinberre, lecturer in English at Girton College, Cambridge, and author of *Shakespeare and the Nature of Women*, offers an insightful and informative analysis of the boy actors and their relationship to the adult male actors of the company. She then explores the particular dynamics of this relationship when the boy actor who plays Kate is given the opportunity to command center stage in the final scene of the play. The boy actor delivers a speech on submission, which is appropriate since the boy actor is in fact subservient to the master actor. Nevertheless, by commanding center stage for his speech, the boy actor upstages the master actor who plays Petruchio. For five minutes the boy playing Kate is the master; his speech steals the show.

Dusinberre postulates that women in the Renaissance audience might have identified with the subordinate actor playing Kate, since they too were subordinate members of society. By identifying with the boy playing Kate, female audience members might also have shared the exhilarating fantasy of "having the last word," of stealing mastery from their husbands, if only for a moment.

The opening of *The Taming of the Shrew* is strikingly different from that of the related play *The Taming of a Shrew* in offering the audience in the first ten lines a battle between the sexes. The Beggar, who calls himself Christopher Sly, threatens to "pheeze" the Hostess who throws him out of her inn, not just for drunkenness, but for not paying for broken

Excerpted from "*The Taming of the Shrew*: Women, Acting, and Power," by Juliet Dusinberre, *Studies in the Literary Imagination*, vol. 26, no. 1 (Spring 1993). Reprinted by permission of the editor of *Studies in the Literary Imagination*, the Georgia State University, Dept. of English.

glasses. Threatening Sly with the stocks, the Hostess exits, determining to send for the constable. In *A Shrew,* the innkeeper is a Tapster, and Slie's offence simply inebriation. Shakespeare's Sly defies the Hostess in a strange little speech: "Ile not budge an inch boy. Let him come, and kindly." He has in the course of eleven lines quoted Kyd's *Spanish Tragedy* and challenged her abuse of him as a rogue: "Y'are a baggage, the Slies are no rogues. Look in the Chronicles, we came in with Richard Conqueror: therefore *paucas pallabris,* let the world slide: Sessa" (*First Folio*). He sounds momentarily like John Durbeyfield in Hardy's *Tess,* claiming an ancient and declining stock. The little interchange offers a vignette in which a man and woman engage in a power struggle: she, only a woman, but with a trade and a function which give her access to authority over him: he a beggar with illusions of grandeur, ancestral memories of great men, culture, a power he no longer possesses. But why does he call her "boy"?

I want to argue that he calls her boy because she is a boy. The Hostess must, in Shakespeare's theatre, have been played by a boy actor. But if Sly addresses her as a boy, then a new dimension is added to the interchange. In his drunkenness he seems momentarily to refuse to enter the play: to be, not a drunken beggar, but a drunken actor, who forgets that his dialogue is with a Hostess, and thinks that the boy actor is getting above himself. In other words, the theatrical illusion seems to be tested before it is even under way. Is Sly a beggar, or is he an actor who must play a beggar?

RELATIONSHIPS BETWEEN ACTORS

In *The Taming of the Shrew,* more than in any other play, Shakespeare uses the relationships between actors as a commentary on the social relationships represented in the self-contained world of the play, the drama of *The Shrew* which is performed before the Beggar (persuaded to believe that he is a lord) at the request of the "real" Lord of the Induction who enters from hunting to refresh himself at the inn and is visited by a company of players. The audience in the theatre is required to react to two competing dramas: a stage representation of a traditional courtship and taming drama; and a more covert drama which constantly interrupts and comments on the taming drama, one generated by the actual structures of relationship present in the company which performs the piece. Sly's use of the term "boy" to the boy actor is only one of many oddities which suggest to the audience the presence in the play itself of actors, not just impersonators of characters. I want to demonstrate how this works in a number of interchanges in the play, and to reinterpret Kate's role in the light of its original theatrical provenance: that Kate would have been played, like the Hostess, Bianca, the Widow, and the young Biondello, by a boy. How would this material condition of Shakespeare's theatre have modified audience perception of the power structures represented in the fiction of *The Taming of the Shrew*?

If Kate is played by a boy in the position of apprentice, then the dynamic between Kate and other players on stage, and between Kate and women in the audience, is altered from what it is in the modern theatre. The boys stood in the position of apprentice towards the adult sharers in the company. It was not a guild apprenticeship, but more of a personal arrangement, such as that between Pepys and his boy Tom Edwards in the 1660s, a child whom he employed as his attendant from the Chapel Royal: well-educated and a good singer. The boys in Shakespeare's company would each have had a particular master; Burbage was master to Nicholas Tooley, and Augustine Phillips—another boy in the company—spoke in his will of Tooley as his "fellow" in the company. The master-pupil relationship between the apprentices and the adult actors and sharers in the company is a highly significant one in the dynamics of the company and can be seen to be in operation in *The Shrew*. The Lord sends instructions to his page on how to play the lady, as any master might have instructed his apprentice on how to play Kate. Furthermore, the apprentice's role in the company creates for him a special relationship with the women in the theatre audience. He must, when the play is done, return to a position of dependency. But great ladies enjoyed a position of social superiority to that of apprentices. The apprentice has within the world of the play access not only to that momentary social superiority but also access to the stage power of the female heroine. Women in the theatre audience may return to the subservient lives of women in Elizabethan social structures, but they too have been allowed within the theatre the fantasy of different kinds of power which link them in sympathy with the boy himself as he represents women on stage. . . .

MASTER ACTORS INSTRUCT SUBORDINATES

In Shakespeare's play, the Lord is emphatically never one of the boys: he is an instructor of boys, both those he would call boy because they are his social inferiors, Sly, the player who must not spoil the show by laughing—and those who really are boys—Bartholomew the page who must play Sly's lady; he calls to one of his men:

> Sirrah, go you to Barthol'mew my page
> And see him dressed in all suits like a lady
> That done, conduct him to the drunkard's chamber,
> And call him "madam", do him obeisance.
> Tell him from me—as he will win my love—
> He bear himself with honourable action
> Such as he hath observed in noble ladies
> Unto their lords, by them accomplished.

He not only advises on the idiom, how the boy is to behave and speak, but on practical matters, how he is to produce tears:

> And if the boy have not a woman's gift
> To rain a shower of commanded tears,
> An onion will do well for such a shift,
> Which in a napkin being close conveyed
> Shall in despite enforce a watery eye.

He is confident that all will be satisfactorily performed:

> I know the boy will well usurp the grace,
> Voice, gait and action of a gentlewoman.

In the next scene he instructs Sly: to be a lord requires a mind stocked with poetry and luxury, hawking and hunting, the arts and music, and the ideal. Sly is beguiled by the language of birth, the imaginative world which opens before him: "I smell sweet savours and I feel soft things." When the Lady enters, she plays her part to perfection:

> My husband and my lord, my lord and husband,
> I am your wife in all obedience.

Does she, one might ask, overplay it a little? Sly announces that he seems to have slept fifteen years, and the Lady responds:

> Ay, and the time seems thirty unto me,
> Being all this time abandoned from your bed.

The effect is instantaneous:

> Sly: 'Tis much. Servants, leave me and her alone.
> Madam, undress you and come now to bed.

If this is a page acting, one suspects that he willfully overplayed his part to make the onlookers laugh. The moment has the zest of purest amateurism: a naughty boy let loose in a woman's clothes, pushing his luck as far as it will go. . . .

THE REWARDS OF PLAYING KATE

The incentive offered to the apprentice who plays Kate is not just the winning of his master's love—and the satisfaction of an actor like Burbage must been worth winning—but his own pride of place in the play. Stage power appears here, even if the price of it is a speech on social submission. Furthermore, behind the text of Kate's obedience speech is the powerful evocation of manhood: dangerous, challenging, adventurous, painful. As the apprentice enters the woman's discourse, the dramatist has seen to it that he conjures up a vision of his own entry into the position of master: the one who takes the risks. But this is also mirrored in his stage situation, because the play stands or falls on the apprentice's performance in the last scene, just as Petruchio's wager stands or falls, and as the husbands gather round to witness their wives' performance, so the masters gather round to see whose apprentice will play the big part: the one with the cloak, the one who studied it first, or the one that the author thought would speak it best. One of the reasons why *The Shrew*, with its apparently time-bound folk-origin conservative dogmas about women, has not simply died a quiet death like all the other Elizabethan plays in the taming genre, is that it releases into the auditorium an energy created through a dialectic of opposed wills, command versus obedience, and power versus powerlessness, which is polarised in the utterance of the boy actor playing the woman.

In *The Taming of the Shrew*, the apprentice has virtually the last word. As the stage heroine mouths obedience, the apprentice eyes his female audience, both the querulous wives on the stage and the women in the audience. Did the women in the audience register the exhilaration of the apprentice actor seizing his chance to be master, to realise stage power even if the price of it was a recognition of the submission to which he and they would have to return once the play was over? The triumph of *The Shrew* is the triumph of art over life, of making a beggar believe that he is part of the play, or of making a drunken actor enter an illusory world and use its language. Men and women in the theatre audience in Shakespeare's play become the watcher, Sly, and take his place as witnesses of the play, but also become seduced, as the Beggar is, into entering the play world, believing it to be real, as the ladies believed Burbage's acting to be real. In this play, Shakespeare has allowed the apprentice to upstage the master, perhaps originally Burbage himself. No one bothers much about Petruchio's reality because they are so busy talking about Kate's. Her speech steals the show. Beneath an ostensible message of humility it generates the suppressed exhilaration of its stage power: the seizing of mastery by the apprentice even as he proclaims a master's doctrine of subjection.

Shakespeare Modifies Folktale Material

Leah Scragg

Leah Scragg is a literary critic whose books on
Shakespeare include *The Metamorphosis of "Gal-
lathea": A Study in Creative Adaptation* and *Shakespeare's Mouldy Tales: Recurrent Plot Motifs in
Shakespearian Drama*. In *Shakespeare's Mouldy
Tales*, Scragg reviews the tradition of taming the
shrew as it is presented in both dramas and non-
dramatic works throughout the medieval and Tudor
periods. She then skillfully reveals how Shakespeare
both uses and transforms the character type and the
taming plot in his own plays.

In this selection Scragg summarizes two folktales that
illustrate the taming of the shrew tradition, then compares
Shakespeare's shrew, Kate, and Shakespeare's shrew-
taming plot with the prototypes in these folklore sources.
Scragg concludes that Kate is more sympathetic and complex than the folklore sources' shrews and that Shakespeare uses the character of the shrew as a means of dis-
cussing a larger theme: social inversion. Undermining
social order is a universal human tendency, Scragg claims,
represented by the shrew. Consequently, taming a shrew
becomes in Shakespeare's play both an exploration of this
human tendency and a lesson for society about the importance of harmonious social relationships.

To the late twentieth-century playgoer, accustomed to a concept of sexual equality enshrined in law if not yet fully em-
braced in practice, probably the least acceptable of the 'tales'
on which Shakespeare draws in the course of his comedies
is that involving the 'taming' of a domineering woman, or
'scold'. Distasteful as this material may appear to the majority of modern readers, the appetite for such stories stretches

back to classical times, while the battle between the sexes, often involving the physical correction of a 'shrew', was a popular motif in both dramatic and non-dramatic literature throughout the medieval and Tudor periods. Since the supremacy of the male constituted an integral part of the theological and social structure that the Renaissance inherited from the Middle Ages, the assertive wife was regarded in the sixteenth and seventeenth centuries not merely as disruptive of marital harmony, but as a threat to the natural order, and her subjugation was consequently posited as a highly desirable end. As both a grammar school boy reared on Roman New Comedy, and an avid reader of contemporary fiction, Shakespeare would have been familiar with the 'scolds' of classical literature and the 'shrews' of folk tales from his boyhood, and it is hardly surprising that the figure of the 'termagant' [aggressive figure of either sex] should have found her way (along with other traditional characters) into his earliest plays. . . .

Two Shrew-Taming Folk Tales

The Kate/Petruchio plot which gives the comedy its title clearly has its origins in the body of folk tales mentioned at the start of this chapter turning on the subjugation of an overbearing wife. Over four hundred versions of the story are extant, but two variations will suffice here to illustrate the tradition to which the play belongs. *A Merry Jest of a Shrewde and Curste Wyfe, Lapped in Morrelles Skin, for Her Good Behavyour* (c. 1550) is typical of the genre. A father (himself married to a shrewish wife), has two daughters, the elder overbearing like her mother, the younger pliant and good natured. The younger daughter, who has many admirers, marries and plays no further part in the tale, while the elder, who has only one suitor, becomes the focus of attention. The father attempts to dissuade her wooer from what he regards as an unwise match, but the young man persists with the courtship, and the marriage takes place. After a lapse of time, the wife's shrewish disposition begins to manifest itself, at which point the husband has his horse, Morrel, slaughtered, and orders its carcass to be flayed. Having forced his wife into a cellar, he beats her to the point of collapse, and then encloses her, naked, in the horse's hide. When she regains consciousness, her body stinging with the salt with which the animal's skin had previously been sprinkled, her husband threatens to keep her enclosed in the hide for the remainder of her life—thus effecting an immediate change in her attitude towards him. The husband then invites his parents-in-law to visit them, and exhibits the submissiveness of his wife, outraging his mother-in-law, who is promptly informed by her daughter that she too would have learnt obedience had she been wrapped in Morrel's skin.

The Handsome Lazy Lass constitutes a variation on this kind of story in that a rather less brutal form of taming is employed. Here the wife's character is flawed by laziness, and the husband brings about the requisite improvement in her conduct by having his own food served to his hard-working servants, and reserving inferior fare for his own table. Recognizing that industry brings tangible rewards, the wife quickly abandons her antisocial conduct, volunteering for the most arduous tasks. Satisfied of her reformation, her husband then reverses his former instructions, allowing her the food appropriate to her rank.

It will be obvious to anyone familiar with the plot of *The Taming of the Shrew* that the play is heavily dependent on the tradition to which these tales belong, and that it draws upon both their physical and psychological methods of taming. The Shakespearian version of the story opens with the father's announcement that he will not consent to the marriage of his younger daughter, Bianca, until a husband has been found for her shrewish sister, Katherina. The arrival of the bold and wayward Petruchio in search of a rich wife provides a potential solution to this difficulty, and encouraged by Bianca's suitors he proceeds to woo, and eventually marry, Katherina. Determined to reduce her from a vixen to a dutiful wife, he decides to overgo her intemperance by the violence and irrationality of his own behaviour. He thus arrives for the wedding in clothes grotesquely inappropriate to the occasion, swears during the ceremony, strikes the priest, and throws wine over the sexton. He then insists on leaving the assembled company before the wedding breakfast, forcing his newly married wife to endure considerable physical hardship on her way to her new home. Once arrived there, he refuses her food on the grounds that the meal served to them is burned, denies her rest by finding fault with the making of the bed, and rejects the new clothes that have been made for her on the grounds that they are unfit to wear. Reduced to a condition of misery and exhaustion, Kate is forced to recognize the discord that will result from the crossing of his will, and consequently resolves to defer to his wishes. From the last scene of Act IV it is thus his will that governs her actions. She declares the sun to be the moon at his instigation, salutes an old man as a young virgin, tramples on her own cap in front of her father's household, and finally delivers a lecture to her fellow wives, at his command, on the duty that married women owe to their husbands.

Popular as such exemplary stories were in the sixteenth century, the kind of plot outlined above is patently not one likely to recommend itself to a contemporary audience. Not only is the assumed ideal on which it depends at variance with twentieth-century attitudes towards the relationship between the sexes, but the conduct of the husband in asserting his authority repels by its brutality rather than engaging admiration or respect. The play as outlined above lends itself to feminist readings, and is frequently discussed in terms of the oppressive nature of patriarchal institutions. In fact, however, though the treatment that Kate receives from Petruchio smacks of the systematic cruelty of the 'Morrel' tale, Shakespeare does not present an unmodified version of the taming process. By adding to his inherited material he places the figure of the scold within a highly complex framework, simultaneously qualifying the audience's response to the central figures, while deepening the significance of the fabliaux [humorous, bawdy story] material on which he draws.

Though contemporary criticism of the play has tended to centre on the persons of the 'shrew' plot, in fact, it is not Kate and Petruchio with whom the members of the audience are first presented on taking their seats in the theatre. The play opens with an altercation between the 'hostess' of a tavern and a tinker named Sly, and it is upon the second of these characters that attention is focused in the opening scenes. The hostess having left in search of a constable, Sly falls into a drunken sleep, and is thus unaware of the arrival of a Lord and his followers, who decide to dress him up as a nobleman, and to enjoy his confusion at his translated state. This plan having been effected, a company of players present themselves at the Lord's house, and are requested to perform a play for his 'noble' guest. At the same time, the Lord instructs his page to disguise himself as a woman and to present himself to the tinker as his wife, while he himself waits on Sly in the guise of a servant. The play which is then begun (of which the shrew plot forms one strand) is consequently not, at this stage, the primary focus of audience attention. It is Sly who has been the central interest from the outset, and his responses with which the spectator is engaged when the characters played by the travelling actors are introduced. Shakespeare's Kate is thus first perceived by the theatre audience not as a 'real' person, but as a character in a play within a play, and is distanced from the spectator by the intervention of an internal audience between those outside the play world and the inset drama.

THE THEME OF SOCIAL INVERSION

The scenes involving Sly do not simply serve, however, to impose a degree of distance between the spectators and the 'shrew' play, reducing the 'reality' of the action that they frame. They also introduce the themes of the central interest, and engineer a stance towards the events that are enacted. The Induction is concerned throughout with social inversion. It begins with a confrontation between the sexes, in which a blustering male is worsted by a woman. Having lapsed into a drunken sleep, Sly undergoes a further decline from man to beast, only to be elevated through the intervention of the Lord from his true position in the social order to an inappropriately high one. At the same time, the Lord becomes a servant, and his page a woman, with the result that the 'shrew' play is performed, not before a conventional court, but in a topsyturvy world. This confused environment has, moreover, a dreamlike quality. Sly himself is unsure whether he is awake or asleep, cf:

> Am I a lord, and have I such a lady?
> Or do I dream? Or have I dream'd till now?

while the Lord suggests that Sly's brief period of ennoblement (during which the inset drama takes place) will later seem to him like a 'flatt'ring dream'. At the same time, this inverted, unreal world is the product of 'game.' The Lord has instigated Sly's metamorphosis into an aristocrat for 'pastime,' and his followers enter into the device with enthusiasm, deriving considerable amusement from the prospect of playing their parts. The comedy performed by the travelling players is thus set in the context of courtly fun, adding a further dimension at its inception to the licensed misrule instituted in an aristocratic household as a means of passing a winter's day.

It will be apparent from the above that the scenes involving Sly are designed to soften the hard outlines of the principal action in a number of ways. The play within a play structure establishes the inset drama as art rather than life, while the social relationships that the shrew play projects function both as an aspect of Sly's dream, and as an extension of the species of Bacchanalia [riotous festivity] that is in progress in the Lord's household. It is not merely the intervention of the frame plot between the theatre audience and the play proper, however, that points to a more sophisticated treatment of the shrew theme than a summary of the story line suggests. The courtship of Kate and Petruchio is paralleled by the attempts of a number of suitors to gain the hand of Baptista's younger daughter, Bianca, and this plot is thematically related to both the Induction and the wooing of Kate. In the first place, the concern with role playing, initiated in the frame plot, invades every aspect of the drama. just as Sly becomes a lord, while the Lord becomes a servant, so in the Bianca plot Tranio, Lucentio's servant, plays the part of his master, rich suitors disguise themselves as tutors, and a pedant assumes the role of a wealthy man. The overbearing conduct and aggressive masculinity of Katherina is thus placed in the context of an entire community in which roles have been exchanged or subverted. Far from being the single aberrant source of discord within a patriarchal society restored to order by her taming, Kate emerges as symptomatic both of the universe in which she exists, and the upside down world in which the comedy is played.

The closing scene of the drama also serves to underline the typicality, as opposed to the idiosyncratic nature, of Kate's conduct. The characters of both strands of the action come together for a banquet (traditionally representative of the restoration of harmony), but it soon becomes apparent that the relations between the members of the social group are far from ideal. The sexes jar both with one another and between themselves, while it quickly emerges that two of the three marriages made in the course of the play contain the seeds of future dissension. Hortensio, who has married a rich widow, is clearly afraid of his wife's anger, while Lucentio, who has won the hand of Bianca, is disappointed in his expectation that she will automatically comply with his will. Kate's defective relations with those around her are thus not the sole target of criticism. Rather than being exclusive to her own situation, her shrewishness is an instance

of universal phenomenon, the tendency of human beings—
male and female—to undermine, through their 'froward-
ness', the orderly functioning of the social group.

KATE IS DEPICTED SYMPATHETICALLY

While the treatment of Bianca and her suitors suggests the
typicality of Kate's conduct, the handling of the shrew herself is much more sympathetic than in the sources from
which the play's action derives. Unlike the conventional
scold, who is arrogant and self-assertive by nature, Kate is
supplied with an explanation for her conduct—and one that
reflects adversely on those around her. She first appears
with her father and her sister's suitors, and the treatment
that she receives invites her resentment of both:

> BAP[TISTA]. Gentlemen, importune me no farther,
>   For how I firmly am resolv'd you know;
>   That is, not to bestow my youngest daughter
>   Before I have a husband for the elder.
>   If either of you both love Katherina,
>   Because I know you well and love you well,
>   Leave shall you have to court her at your pleasure.
> GRE[MIO]. To cart her rather. She's too rough for me.
>   There, there, Hortensio, will you any wife?
> KATH. I pray you, sir, is it your will
>   To make a stale of me amongst these mates?
> HOR[TENSIO]. Mates, maid, how mean you that? no mates for you
>   Unless you were of gentler, milder mould.

Here the rebuke that she delivers to her father is justified by
his failure to protect her from abuse, while the contempt that
she exhibits for her suitors is warranted by the rudeness of
their behaviour. Similarly, though it appears at first sight that
her hostility towards Bianca is motivated solely by the universal preference for the younger woman, there are a number of indications that her resentment also derives from the
knowledge that the assumptions made about her sister are
ill-founded. The action of the play, moreover, bears out the
implication that Bianca's disposition is not what it appears to
be. Though Lucentio, on first seeing the sisters, assumes that
appearance and reality coincide—i.e. that one is a termagant,
and the other the embodiment of 'mild behaviour and sobriety'—as the comedy unfolds both the members of the audience and Lucentio himself are obliged to revise this assess-
ment. Bianca shows herself capable of being as peremptory
as her sister in her conduct towards her 'tutors,' while at the

close of the play she declines to come at her husband's command, rejecting the dutifulness displayed by Kate towards Petruchio in terms that bode ill for her own marriage:

> BIAN. Fie, what a foolish duty call you this?
> LUC. I would your duty were as foolish too.
>   The wisdom of your duty, fair Bianca,
>   Hath cost me a hundred crowns since supper-time.
> BIAN. The more fool you for laying on my duty.

MISOGYNISTIC FOLK TALE MATERIAL TRANSFORMED

It is the ultimate status achieved by the central figure, however, that constitutes Shakespeare's most significant adaptation of his inherited material. At the outset of the action it is clearly established that Kate's behaviour, warranted though it may be, is prejudicial not only to the community at large but to her own happiness. She is disrespectful towards her father, cruel to her sister, and hostile both to Bianca's suitors and to the single aspirant to her own hand. Her adverse effect upon the social group is reflected in the extreme responses that she elicits from those around her. Her father refers to her as a 'hilding of a devilish spirit,' while her sister's suitors variously regard her as 'rough,' 'intolerable curst,' and 'shrewd, and froward . . . beyond all measure.' She is thus presented as an isolated figure existing in a society governed by assumptions which she rejects, and it might appear at first sight that the action of the play merely brings her from violent opposition to her world to an enforced conformity with its mercantile values and hierarchical structures. In fact, Kate's progress may be more adequately described as a process of education that leaves her essential spirit unchanged, but transforms her relationship with those around her. It is clear from the outset that although Petruchio's motivation in pursuing the match is initially financial, he is also intrigued and impressed by the spirit that his prospective bride exhibits. On being told, for example, that she has broken a lute over the head of one of her tutors, he exclaims:

> Now, by the world, it is a lusty wench.
> I love her ten times more than e'er I did.

This appreciation of a strength of character equal to his own carries with it the promise of a more valuable relationship developing between the couple than Petruchio's pecuniary aspirations initially suggest, and it is the growth of this understanding, for all the physicality of the action through

which it evolves, that the play traces. The course of conduct
that Petruchio pursues—violating the decorum of the marriage ceremony, refusing to attend the wedding breakfast,
subjecting his newly married wife to a long and arduous
journey, depriving her of food, rest and new clothes on the
pretence that nothing is too good for her—not only affords
Kate a mirror image of her own behaviour, but brings her to
recognize her own dependence on the orderly conduct of
day-to-day life, and on the conventions she had previously
scorned. While Bianca learns nothing from her succession
of tutors, Kate is thus educated into a fuller awareness of her
own priorities, while becoming more considerate of others
through sharing the miseries to which intemperance and
the abuse of authority lead. At the same time, she evolves a
relationship with her husband that is more than a *modus
vivendi* [way of living]. The turning point in this process occurs during the return journey to Baptista's house, when she
contradicts Petruchio for the last time over the seemingly in-
controvertible question of the time of day:

> PET. Good Lord, how bright and goodly shines the moon!
> KATH. The moon? The sun! It is not moonlight now.
> PET. I say it is the moon that shines so bright.
> KATH. I know it is the sun that shines so bright.
> PET. Now by my mother's son, and that's myself,
>   It shall be moon, or star, or what I list,
>   Or e'er I journey to your father's house.
> [*To Servants.*] Go on, and fetch our horses back again.—
>   Evermore cross'd and cross'd, nothing but cross'd.

Recognizing that the journey will be abandoned unless he
has his way, Kate elects to defer to him, not only on this
point, but on any other position he cares to assume:

> KATH. Forward, I pray, since we have come so far,
>   And be it moon, or sun, or what you please.
>   And if you please to call it a rush-candle,
>   Henceforth I vow it shall be so for me.

Given the privations she has endured prior to this scene, and
her anxiety to return to her father's house, this response
might well be interpreted as representing the conventional
cowing of the shrew to her husband's will. The encounter
with Vincentio that follows, however, immediately qualifies
this impression. Petruchio salutes the old man as a woman,
inviting Kate to do the same, and is met, not with sullen acquiescence, but with a spirited entry into the game he has
determined to play:

PET. [*To Vincentio.*] Good morrow, gentle mistress, where away?
   Tell me, sweet Kate, and tell me truly too,
   Hast thou beheld a fresher gentlewoman?
   Such war of white and red within her cheeks!
   What stars do spangle heaven with such beauty
   As those two eyes become that heavenly face?
   Fair lovely maid, once more good day to thee.
   Sweet Kate, embrace her for her beauty's sake.
   . . . .

KATH. Young budding virgin, fair and fresh, and sweet,
   Whither away, or where is thy abode?
   Happy the parents of so fair a child,
   Happier the man whom favourable stars
   Allots thee for his lovely bedfellow!
PET. Why, how now, Kate, I hope thou art not mad.
   This is a man, old, wrinkled, faded, wither'd,
   And not a maiden, as thou say'st he is.
KATH. Pardon, old father, my mistaking eyes,
   That have been so bedazzled with the sun
   That everything I look on seemeth green.
   Now I perceive thou art a reverend father.
   Pardon, I pray thee, for my mad mistaking.

Clearly, the Kate who speaks these lines is not a broken woman, but one who has learnt to accommodate her spirit and strength of will to the situation in which she is placed. The tone in which she speaks is suggested by Vincentio's subsequent reference to her as a 'merry mistress' and this sense of shared merriment between the central couple is confirmed at the end of the exchange, and carried forward into the final act. In the closing scene while divisions are exposed between the parallel couples (Lucentio and Bianca / Hortensio and the Widow), Petruchio and Kate operate in partnership, and it is they who finally emerge as the upholders of the social order. Faced with the recalcitrant attitudes of Bianca and the Widow, Petruchio charges Kate to bring the offending wives before their husbands, and it is she who instructs those who had formerly repudiated her on the attitudes that make for harmonious relationships within the social group. In the topsyturvy world of the 'shrew' play it is thus the 'scold' who achieves marital happiness, while the initial object of male admiration falls short of the conventional ideal. . . .

The Taming of the Shrew transforms the misogynistic material of popular tradition into a vehicle for the exploration of a universal tendency, overturning audience expectations by its final alignment with the central figure.

CHAPTER 3

Critical
Interpretations

The Spirit of Farce in *The Taming of the Shrew*

Robert B. Heilman

Robert B. Heilman, a scholar and professor for over
half a century, has published several books on Shakespeare's tragedies and since 1965 has served on the
advisory board for the journal *Shakespeare Studies.*
Heilman has also written an introduction to *The Taming of the Shrew* for the Signet edition of the play.
   In this article Heilman identifies the elements of farce in
The Taming of the Shrew. Farce classifies works of literature in which characters are limited and mechanical and
action is fast-paced. Practical jokes, improbable situations,
and sudden transformations also characterize farce. Heilman explains, for example, that Petruchio's successful taming of Kate, in a week, as if she were a falcon would be improbable in real life; as an example of "the farcical view of
life," though, the taming works as smoothly as an established training routine. The audience appreciates the quick
and total apparent change and does not wonder how the
characters feel or if a person would really behave as Kate
and Petruchio do, Heilman claims. It is to Shakespeare's
credit, Heilman concludes, that he could achieve so much
within the limited genre of farce.

We tend to take farce simply as hurly-burly theater, with
much slapstick, roughhouse (Petruchio with a whip, as in
the older productions), pratfalls, general confusion, trickery,
uproars, gags, practical jokes, and so on. Yet such character-
istics, which often do appear in farce, are surface manifestations. What we need to identify is the "spirit of farce"
which lies behind them. We should then be able to look
more discerningly at *The Taming*—to see in what sense it is
a farce, and what it does with the genre of farce.

Excerpted from "The Taming Untamed; or, The Return of the Shrew," by Robert B.
Heilman, *Modern Language Quarterly*, vol. 27, no. 2 (June 1976). Copyright ©1976,
University of Washington. Reprinted by permission of Duke University Press.

THE GENRE OF FARCE

A genre is a conventionalized way of dealing with actuality, and different genres represent different habits of the human mind, or minister to the human capacity for finding pleasure in different styles of artistic representation. "Romance," for instance, is the genre which conceives of obstacles, dangers, and threats, especially those of an unusual or spectacular kind, as yielding to human ingenuity, spirit, or just good luck. On the other hand "naturalism," as a literary mode, conceives of man as overcome by the pressure of outer forces, especially those of a dull, grinding persistence. The essential procedure of farce is to deal with people as if they lack, largely or totally, the physical, emotional, intellectual, and moral sensitivity that we think of as "normal." The undying popularity of farce for several thousand years indicates that, though "farce" is often a term of disparagement, a great many people, no doubt all of us at times, take pleasure in seeing human beings acting as if they were very limited human beings. Farce offers a spectacle that resembles daily actuality but lets us participate without feeling the responsibilities and liabilities that the situation would normally evoke. Perhaps we feel superior to the diminished men and women in the plot; perhaps we harmlessly work off aggressions (since verbal and physical assaults are frequent in farce). Participation in farce is easy on us; in it we escape the full complexity of our own natures and cut up without physical or moral penalties. Farce is the realm without pain or conscience. Farce offers a holiday from vulnerability, consequences, costs. It is the opposite of all the dramas of disaster in which a man's fate is too much for him. It carries out our persistent if unconscious desire to simplify life by a selective anaesthetizing of the whole person; in farce, man retains all his energy yet never gets really hurt. The give-and-take of life becomes a brisk skirmishing in which one needs neither health insurance nor liability insurance; when one is on the receiving end and has to take it, he bounces back up resiliently, and when he dishes it out, his pleasure in conquest is never undercut by the guilt of inflicting injury.

FAST-PACED ACTION

In farce, the human personality is without depth. Hence action is not slowed down by thought or by the friction of competing motives. Everything goes at high speed, with dash, variety, never a pause for stocktaking, and ever an athlete's quick glance ahead at the action coming up next. No sooner do the Players come in than the Lord plans a show to help bamboozle Sly. As soon as Baptista appears with his daughters and announces the marriage priority, other lovers plan to find a man for Kate, Lucentio falls in love with Bianca and hits on an approach in disguise, Petruchio plans to go for Kate, Bianca's lovers promise him support, Petruchio begins his suit and introduces Hortensio into the scramble of disguised lovers. Petruchio rushes through the preliminary business with Baptista and the main business with Kate, and we have a marriage. The reader is hurried over the rivalries of Bianca's lovers, making their bids to Baptista and appealing directly to the girl herself, back to Kate's wedding-day scandals and out into the country for the postmarital welter of disturbances; then we shift back and forth regularly from rapid action in the Kate plot to almost equally rapid action in the Bianca plot. And so on. The driving pace made possible, and indeed necessitated, by the absence of depth is brilliantly managed.

In the absence of depth one is not bothered by distractions; in fact, what are logically distractions are not felt as such if they fit into the pattern of carefree farcical hammer and tongs, cut and thrust. At Petruchio's first appearance the "knocking at the gate" confusion is there for fun, not function. The first hundred lines between Grumio and Curtis are a lively rattle, full of the verbal and physical blows of farce, but practically without bearing on the action. Kate is virtually forgotten for sixty lines as Petruchio and Grumio fall into their virtuoso game of abusing the tailor. Furthermore, action without depth has a mechanical, automatic quality: when two Vincentios appear, people do not reason about the duplication, but, frustrated by confusion and bluffing, quickly have recourse to blows and insults, accusations of madness and chicanery, and threats of arrest—standard procedures in farce from Plautus on. Vincentio's "Thus strangers may be halèd and abused" is not a bad description of the manners of farce, in which incapacity to sort things out is basic. Mechanical action, in turn, often tends to symmetrical effects: the lovers of Kate and Bianca first bargain with Baptista, then approach the girls; Hortensio and Tranio (as Lucentio) resign their claims to Bianca in almost choral fashion; Bianca and the Widow (Hortensio's new spouse) respond identically to the requests of their husbands. In this final scene we have striking evidence of the manipulation of personality in the interest of symmetrical effect. Shakespeare unmistakably wants a double reversal of role at the end, a symmetry of converse movements. The new Kate has developed out of a shrew, so the old Bianca must develop into a shrew. The earlier treatment of her hardly justifies sudden transformation, immediately after marriage, into a cool, offhand, recalcitrant, even challenging wife. Like many another character in farce, she succumbs to the habits of the generic form. Yet some modern critics treat her as harshly as if from the start she were a particularly obnoxious female.

Limited, Mechanical Characters

All these effects come from a certain arbitrarily limited sense of personality. Those who have this personality are not really hurt, do not think much, are not much troubled by scruples. Farce often turns on practical jokes, in which the sadistic impulse is not restrained by any sense of injury to the victim. It would never occur to anyone that Sly might be pained or humiliated by acting as a Lord and then being let down. No one hesitates to make rough jokes about Kate (even calling her "fiend of hell") in her hearing. No one putting on a disguise to dupe others has any ethical inhibitions; the end always justifies the means. When Kate "breaks the lute to" Hortensio, farce requires that he act terrified; but it does not permit him to be injured or really resentful or grieved by the loss of the lute, as a man in a nonfarcical world might well be. Verbal abuse is almost an art form; it does not hurt, as it would in ordinary life. No one supposes that the victims of Petruchio's manhandling and tantrums—the priest and sexton at the wedding, the servants and tradesmen at his home—really feel the outrageous treatment that they get. When Petruchio and Hortensio call "To her" to Kate and the Widow, it is like starting a dogfight or cockfight. Petruchio's order to Kate to bring out the other wives is like having a trained dog retrieve a stick. The scene is possible because one husband and three wives are not endowed with full human personalities; if they were, they simply could not function as trainer, retriever, and sticks.

In identifying the farcical elements in *The Shrew,* we have gradually shifted from the insensitivity that the characters must have to the mechanicalness of their responses. These people rarely think, hesitate, deliberate, or choose; they act just as quickly and unambiguously as if someone had pressed a control button. Farce simplifies life by making it not only painless but also automatic; indeed, the two qualities come together in the concept of man as machine. There is a sense in which we might legitimately call the age of computers a farcical one, for it lets us feel that basic choices are made without mental struggle or will or anxiety, and as speedily and inevitably as a series of human ninepins falling down one after other on the stage when each is bumped by the one next to it. "Belike you mean," says Kate to Petruchio, "to make a puppet of me." It is what farce does to all characters.

TAMING AS FALCON TRAINING

Now the least obvious and at the same time most fundamental illustration of the farcical view of life lies not in some of the peripheral goings on that we have been observing, but in the title action itself: the taming of the shrew. Essentially—we will come shortly to the necessary qualifications—Kate is conceived of as responding automatically to a certain kind of calculated treatment, as automatically as an animal to the devices of a skilled trainer. Petruchio not only uses the word *tame* more than once, but openly compares his method to that used in training falcons. There is no reason whatever to suppose that this was not meant quite literally. Petruchio is not making a great jest or developing a paradoxical figure but is describing a process taken at face value. He tells exactly what he has done and is doing—withholding food and sleep until the absolute need of them brings assent. . . . Before he sees Kate, he explicitly announces his method: he will assert, as true, the opposite of whatever she says and does and is, that is to say, he will frustrate the manifestations of her will and establish the dominance of his own. Without naming them, he takes other steps that we know to be important in animal training. From the beginning he shows that he will stop at nothing to achieve his end, that he will not hesitate for a second to do anything necessary—to discard all dignity or carry out any indecorous act or any outrageousness that will serve. He creates an image of utter invincibility, of having no weakness through which he can be appealed to. He does not use a literal whip, such as stage Petruchios habitually used, but he unmistakably uses a symbolic whip. Like a good trainer, however, he uses the carrot as well as the whip—not only marriage, but a new life, a happier personality for Kate. Above all, he offers love; in the end, the trainer succeeds best who makes the trainee feel the presence of something warmer than technique, rigor, and invincibility. Not that Petruchio fakes love, but that love has its part, ironically, in a process that is farcically conceived and that never wholly loses the markings of farce.

KATE'S SUDDEN TRANSFORMATION

Only in farce could we conceive of the occurrence, almost in a flash, of that transformation of personality which, as we know only too well in modern experience, normally requires a long, gradual, painstaking application of psychotherapy. True, conversion is believable and does happen, but even as a secular experience it requires a prior development of readiness, or an extraordinary revelatory shock, or both. . . . Kate is presented initially as a very troubled woman; aggressiveness and tantrums are her way of feeling a sense of power. Though modern, the argument that we see in her the result of paternal unkindness is not impressive. For one thing, some recent [1966] research on infants—if we may risk applying heavy science to light farce—suggests that basic personality traits precede, and perhaps influence, parental attitudes to children. More important, the text simply does not present Baptista as the overbearing and tyrannical father that he is sometimes said to be. Kate has made him almost as unhappy as she is, and driven him toward Bianca; nevertheless, when he heavily handicaps Bianca in the matrimonial sweepstakes, he is trying to even things up for the daughter who he naturally thinks is a poor runner. Nor is he willing to marry her off to Petruchio simply to get rid of her; "her love," he says, "is all in all." On her wedding day he says, kindly enough, "I cannot blame thee now to weep," and at the risk of losing husbands for both daughters he rebukes Petruchio. . . . We cannot blacken Baptista to save Kate. Shakespeare presents her binding and beating Bianca to show that he is really committed to a shrew; such episodes make it hard to defend the view that she is an innocent victim or is posing as a shrew out of general disgust.

AS FARCE, THE TAMING IS BELIEVABLE

To sum up: in real life her disposition would be difficult to alter permanently, but farce secures its pleasurable effect by assuming a ready and total change in response to the stimuli applied by Petruchio as if he were going through an established and proved training routine. On the other hand, only farce makes it possible for Petruchio to be so skillful a tamer, that is, so unerring, so undeviating, so mechanical, so uninhibited an enforcer of the rules for training in falconry. If Petruchio were by nature the disciplinarian that he acts for a while, he would hardly change after receiving compliance; and if he were, in real life, the charming and affectionate gentleman that he becomes in the play, he would find it impossible so rigorously to play the falcon-tamer, to outbully the bully, especially when the bully lies bleeding on the ground, for this role would simply run afoul of too much of his personality. The point here is not that the play is "unrealistic" (this would be a wholly irrelevant criticism), but that we can understand how a given genre works by testing it against the best sense of reality that we can bring to bear. It is the farcical view of life that makes possible the treatment of both Kate and Petruchio.

FARCE EXPANDS TOWARD COMEDY OF CHARACTER

But this picture, of course, is incomplete; for the sake of clarity we have been stressing the purely generic in *The Shrew* and gliding over the specific variations. Like any genre, farce is a convention, not a strait jacket; it is a fashion, capable of many variations. Genre provides a perspective, which in the individual work can be used narrowly or inclusively: comedy of manners, for instance, can move toward the character studies of James's novels or toward the superficial entertainments of Terence Rattigan. Shakespeare hardly ever uses *a* genre constrictively. In both *The Comedy of Errors* and *The Taming of the Shrew,* the resemblances between which are well known, Shakespeare freely alters the limited conception of personality that we find in "basic farce" such as that of Plautus, who influences both these plays. True, he protects both main characters in *The Shrew* against the expectable liabilities that would make one a less perfect reformer, and the other less than a model reformee, but he is unwilling to leave them automatons, textbook types of reformer and reformee. So he equips both with a good deal of intelligence and feeling that they would not have in elementary farce. Take sex, for instance. In basic farce, sex is purely a mechanical response, with no more overtones of feeling than ordinary hunger and thirst; the normal "love affair" is an intrigue with a courtesan. Like virtually all Renaissance lovers, Petruchio tells Kate candidly that he proposes to keep warm "in thy bed." But there is no doubt that Petruchio, in addition to wanting a good financial bargain and enjoying the challenge of the shrew, develops real warmth of feeling for Kate as an individual—a warmth that makes him strive to bring out the best in her, keep the training in a tone of jesting, well-meant fantasy, provide Kate with face-saving devices (she is "curst . . . for policy" and only "in company"), praise her for her virtues (whether she has them or not) rather than blame her for her vices, never fall into boorishness, repeatedly protest his affection for her, and, by asking a kiss at a time she thinks unsuitable, show that he really wants it. Here farce expands toward comedy of character by using a fuller range of personality.

Likewise with Kate. The fact that she is truly a shrew does not mean that she cannot have hurt feelings, as it would in a plainer farce; indeed, a shrew may be defined—once she develops beyond a mere stereotype—as a person who has an excess of hurt feelings and is taking revenge on the world for them. Although we dislike the revenge, we do not deny the painful feelings that may lie behind. Shakespeare has chosen to show some of those feelings, not making Kate an insentient virago on the one hand, or a pathetic victim on the other. She plainly is jealous of Bianca and her lovers; she accuses Baptista of favoritism; on her wedding day she suffers real anguish rather than simply an automatic, conventionally furious resolve for retaliation. The painful emotions take her way beyond the limitations of the essentially pain-free personality of basic farce. Further, she is witty, though, truth to tell, the first verbal battle between her and Petruchio, like various other such scenes, hardly goes beyond verbal farce, in which words are mechanical jokes or blows rather than an artistic game that delights by its quality, and in which all the speed of the short lines hardly conceals the heavy labors of the dutiful but uninspired punster (the best jokes are the bawdy ones). Kate has imagination. It shows first in a new human sympathy when she defends the servants against Petruchio. Then it develops into a gay, inspired gamesomeness that rivals Petruchio's own. When he insists, "It shall be what o'clock I say it is" and "[The sun] shall be moon or star or what I list," he is at one level saying again that he will stop at nothing, at no irrationality, as tamer; but here he moves the power-game into a realm of fancy in which his apparent willfulness becomes the acting of the creative imagination. He is a poet, and he asks her, in effect, less to kiss the rod than to join in the game of playfully transforming ordinary reality. It is the final step in transforming herself. The point here is that, instead of not catching on or simply sulking, Kate has the dash and verve to join in the fun, and to do it with skill and some real touches of originality.

THE ENDING REVERTS TO FARCE

This episode on the road to Padua, when Petruchio and Kate first transform old Vincentio into a "Young budding virgin, fair and fresh and sweet," and then back into himself again, is the high point of the play. From here on, it tends to move back closer to the boundaries of ordinary farce. When Petruchio asks a kiss, we do have human beings with feelings, not robots; but the key line, which is sometimes missed, is Petruchio's "Why, then let's home again. Come, sirrah, let's away." Here Petruchio is again making the same threat that he made at IV.v.8–9, that is, not playing an imaginative game but hinting the symbolic whip, even though the end is a compliance that she is inwardly glad to give. The whole wager scene falls essentially within the realm of farce: the responses are largely mechanical, as is their symmetry. Kate's final long speech on the obligations and fitting style of wives we can think of as a more or less automatic statement—that is, the kind appropriate to farce—of a generally held doctrine. . . .

KATE'S REAL VICTORY

The play gives no evidence that from now on she will be twisting her husband around her finger. The evidence is rather that she will win peace and quiet and contentment by giving in to his wishes, and that her willingness will entirely eliminate unreasonable and autocratic wishes in him. But after all, the unreasonable and the autocratic are his strategy, not his nature; he gives up an assumed vice, while Kate gives up a real one. The truth is that, with Petruchio's help, Kate's great victory is over herself; she has come to accept herself as having enough merit so that she can be content without having the last word and scaring everybody off. To see this means to acknowledge that she was originally a shrew, whatever virtues may also have been latent in her personality.

FARCE AND MORE

What Shakespeare has done is to take an old, popular farcical situation and turn it into a well-organized, somewhat complex, fast-moving farce of his own. He has worked with the basic conceptions of farce—mainly that of a somewhat limited personality that acts and responds in a mechanical way and hence moves toward a given end with a perfection not likely if all the elements in human nature were really at work. So the tamer never fails in his technique, and the shrew responds just as she should. Now this situation might have tempted the dramatist to let his main characters be flat automatons—he a dull and rough whip-wielder and she a stubborn intransigent until beaten into insensibility. . . . Shakespeare, however, makes a gentleman and lady of his central pair. As tamer, Petruchio is a gay and witty and precocious artist and, beyond that, an affectionate man; and hence, a remarkable therapist. In Kate, Shakespeare has imagined not merely a harridan who is incurable or a moral stepchild driven into a misconduct by mistreatment, but a difficult woman—a shrew, indeed—who combines willfulness with feelings that elicit sympathy, with imagination, and with a latent coöperativeness that can bring this war of the sexes to an honorable settlement. To have started with farce, to have stuck to the main lines of farce, and yet to have got so much of the suprafarcical into farce—this is the achievement of *The Taming of the Shrew*, and the source of the pleasure that it has always given.

Romantic Comedy Humanizes the Heroine

John C. Bean

John C. Bean, associate professor of English at Montana State University, has written several articles on the treatment of love in Shakespeare's comedies. He also served as cochair of the 1977 MLA special session on "Marriage and the Family in Shakespeare." Bean argues that Kate is more like the heroines in Shakespeare's later romantic comedies than a mechanical figure from a farce. She is not tamed into submission like the Kate of the anonymous play *The Taming of a Shrew*. Neither is she untamed and simply pretending to be submissive in the final scene. Bean claims that Kate is actually immersed in the chaos of an irrational world by Petruchio's antics. When she discovers laughter, she emerges from this chaotic world as if she were emerging from a dream. The awakened Kate has achieved a new sense of personal identity and has discovered love as a result of the experience. In Bean's view, Kate's final speech is not a vocal submission to male tyranny, but an acknowledgement of the duties of both husbands and wives to each other. Although farcical elements in the play tend to depersonalize Kate, the humanization of this heroine helps us understand both the play and Shakespeare's search for a comic form worthy of his characters.

Much recent criticism of Shakespeare's *The Taming of the Shrew* can be divided into two camps, the revisionists and the anti-revisionists. The revisionists have argued that Kate's notorious last speech is delivered ironically and that Kate, in retaining her psychological independence from the "duped" Petruchio, remains untamed. As seen by the revisionists, *The*

Excerpted from "Comic Structure and the Humanizing of Kate in *The Taming of the Shrew*," by John C. Bean, in *The Woman's Part: Feminist Criticism of Shakespeare*, edited by Carolyn Ruth Swift Lenz et al. Copyright 1980 by Board of Trustees of the University of Illinois. Used with permission of the University of Illinois Press.

Taming of the Shrew is a relatively sophisticated social comedy, the ironic texture of which directs our attention not primarily to Kate's psychological illness but to the social illness of a materialistic patriarchy. The anti-revisionists, on the other hand, insisting on historical accuracy, have argued that Kate is tamed through the reductive procedures of rollicking, old-fashioned farce. In *The Taming of the Shrew,* argues the anti-revisionist Robert B. Heilman, "Kate is conceived of as responding automatically to a certain kind of calculated treatment, as automatically as an animal to the devices of a skilled trainer."

In this essay, I wish to object to both camps—to the revisionists' belief that we should not take Kate's last speech straightforwardly, and to the anti-revisionists' belief that Kate responds in an animallike fashion to Petruchio's taming tactics. What we should emphasize in *The Taming of the Shrew* is the emergence of a humanized heroine against the background of depersonalizing farce unassimilated from the play's fabliau [comic and lewd medieval tale] sources. If we can appreciate the liberal element in Kate's last speech—the speech that strikes modern sensibilities as advocating male tyranny—we can perhaps see that Kate is tamed not in the automatic manner of behavioral psychology but in the spontaneous manner of the later romantic comedies where characters lose themselves in chaos and emerge, as if from a dream, liberated into the bonds of love. I shall not be arguing that the play fits neatly into the genre of romance, for the older farcical elements are continually at odds with the romantic; rather, I shall try to show that the play reveals a relationship between the sophistication of comic structure and the liberation of women from medieval notions of male autocracy. Since farce treats persons as if they lacked the sensitivities of an inward self, that genre is appropriate to a view of marriage in which the wife is mainly the husband's chattel. But Shakespeare's romantic comedy is concerned with the discovery of the inward self, with love as personal, and hence with the relationship of lovers who face together the problem of reconciling liberty and commitment in marriage. Shakespeare's *The Taming of the Shrew* rises from farce to romantic comedy to the exact extent that Kate, in discovering love through the discovery of her own identity, becomes something more than the fabliau stereotype of the shrew turned household drudge. . . .

KATE'S LAST SPEECH

Since I shall be arguing that Shakespeare's play does *not* preach the subjection of women, the place to begin is with Kate's last speech about the duties of wives, a speech that has embarrassed generations of critics. Far from reiterating old platitudes about the inferiority of women, however, what Kate actually says reflects a number of humanist assumptions about an ideal marriage popularized by Tudor matrimonial reformers. If we wish to see a real vision of subjugated woman, we should turn to the parallel speech of Kate in the anonymous *A Shrew*. When Ferando in that play orders Kate to instruct the other wives on their matrimonial duties, she recites a medieval argument about women's moral inferiority, an argument repeated in misogynist tracts at least to the time of Milton.

> Then to his image he did make a man,
> Olde *Adam* and from his side asleepe,
> A rib was taken, of which the Lord did make,
> The woe of man so termd by *Adam* then,
> Woman for that, by her came sinne to us,
> And for her sin was *Adam* doomd to die. . . .

Kate simply gives the Genesis account of woman's responsibility for original sin, her speech emphasizing only the sinfulness and abjection of women. There is nothing in the *A Shrew* version about the husband's duties to the wife or about positive feminine powers such as beauty or nurturing softness; the writer's emphasis is solely on feminine sin. In the *The Shrew* version of the speech, however, Shakespeare makes no reference to moral inferiority in women. His emphasis instead is on reciprocity of duties in marriage, based on the complementary natures of man and woman.

> Fie, fie! unknit that threatening unkind brow,
> And dart not scornful glances from those eyes,
> To wound thy lord, thy king, thy governor:
> It blots thy beauty as frosts do bite the meads,
> Confounds thy fame as whirlwinds shake fair buds,
> And in no sense is meet or amiable.
> A woman mov'd is like a fountain troubled,
> Muddy, ill-seeming, thick, bereft of beauty;
> And while it is so, none so dry or thirsty
> Will deign to sip or touch one drop of it.
> Thy husband is thy lord, thy life, thy keeper,
> Thy head, thy sovereign; one that cares for thee,
> And for thy maintenance commits his body
> To painful labour both by sea and land,

. . . .
And craves no other tribute at thy hands
But love, fair looks, and true obedience;
Too little payment for so great a debt . . .

Here the woman's softness and beauty, in complementing
the man's strength, are affirmative and potent virtues associated with warmth, harmony, peace, and refreshment. Because she now appreciates her own powers, Kate is able to
envision the family as an ordered kingdom in which the
subject's obedience is a response not to the king's will but to
the king's love. The husband is "lord," "governor," "king,"
"sovereign," and the shrewish wife a "foul contending
rebel," a "graceless traitor to her loving lord." "Such duty as
the subject owes the prince, / Even such a woman oweth to
her husband," says Kate, and Petruchio believes that Kate's
acknowledgment of this obedience means "love, and quiet
life, / An awful rule and right supremacy." In our own age,
perhaps, the distinction between matrimonial tyranny and
"right supremacy" is difficult to appreciate, and hence Kate's
speech has been deprecated as antifeminist dogma. But in
the late sixteenth century, an age obsessed with the nature
of ideal kingship and the rightful use of power, such a distinction was important.

THE HUMANIST VIEW OF MARRIAGE

Beginning with the Catholic humanists Erasmus and Juan
Luis Vives and continued by such Protestant reformers as
Heinrich Bullinger and Robert Cleaver, numerous sixteenth-
century writers of matrimonial literature examined the
problem of hierarchy and kingship on the family level. . . .
The problem the matrimonial writers faced was how to rec-
oncile the notion of matrimonial friendship, which tended to
make husband and wife equals, with the notion of hierarchy, which asserted the husband's supremacy. The reconciliation occurs through analogy to the political concept of loving kingship, wherein the prince's love for his people
(analogous in turn to Christ's love for his church) converts
tyranny to harmonious order. Subjects who would rebel
against a tyrant freely serve a loving king. The concept of
loving kingship allows hierarchy without tyranny, for both
the subject and the ruler are bound by the mutual obligations of love. Thus the model for marriage is ultimately political: the family is a miniature kingdom ruled in benevo-

lence by the husband. If the first duty of wives is to obey their husbands, the first duty of husbands, stressed again and again in the domestic books, is to love their wives; and in so loving them husbands relinquish their claims to tyrannical authority and regard their wives as friends rather than as servants. According to Vives "yf a man (as nature, reason, and holy scripture, do saye unto us) be the head of the woman, and Christ the father, there ought to be betwene them such societe and felowship, as is betwene the father and the sonne, and not such as is betwene the maister and the servaunt." The effect of the husband's love is to raise the wife's status from mere drudge to a position of importance and dignity. "Thou shalt not have [thy wife] as a servant . . . but . . . as a most faithful secretary of thy cares and thoughts, and in doubtful matters a wise and a hearty counsellor. This is the true society and fellowship of man. . . .

MUTUAL MARITAL DUTIES

Kate's final speech in *The Shrew,* then, in its use of political analogies and its emphasis on woman's warmth and beauty rather than on her abject sinfulness, is not a rehearsal of old, medieval ideas about wives but of relatively contemporary ideas growing out of humanist reforms. Male tyranny, which characterizes earlier shrew-taming stories, gives way here to a nontyrannical hierarchy informed by mutual affection. In Kate's speech there are no arguments supporting the husband's right to capricious domination nor any recommendation of the wifely submissiveness we find, in say, the patient Griselda [an exceptionally submissive wife in Chaucer's "The Student's Tale"], for Kate's submissiveness depends on Petruchio's "honest will," on his being a "loving lord." Like Cordelia [the loving daughter in *King Lear*], Kate will love only according to her bond, no more, no less, and the limits of her bond will be reached whenever Petruchio's authority ceases to be loving. Within such a marriage model, the wife becomes her husband's friend and companion rather than his faceless drudge so that Kate's last speech, rather than supporting Heilman's contention that the play is farce, opposes the depersonalizing procedure of that genre.

ROMANTIC ELEMENTS IN *THE TAMING*

We are now faced with a new problem: how to interpret Petruchio's taming of Kate in a way consistent with the humanized vision of marriage contained in her last speech. A partial solution is to focus on the fairly consistent pattern of romantic elements in the taming scenes, namely, those elements that show Kate's discovery of her inward self through her discovery first of play and then of love. Such elements look forward to the festive comedies rather than backward to medieval farce, and, although they jar with elements that remain irretrievably farcical, they reveal Shakespeare's conscious attempt to humanize Kate and thereby to achieve a richer comic form.

Let us begin with a reading of Kate's taming that focuses on the romantic elements. If Kate's last speech is not an assertion of male tyranny, as is the equivalent speech in *A Shrew*, there is such an assertion in Shakespeare's play, one as rude as any we find in the medieval misogynist tracts, but it occurs significantly in Act III before Kate is tamed while Petruchio is playing his preposterous role at the first wedding feast.

> Nay, look not big, nor stamp, nor stare, nor fret;
> I will be master of what is mine own.
> She is my goods, my chattels; she is my house,
> My household stuff, my field, my barn,
> My horse, my ox, my ass, my anything.

Here is the harsh doctrine of male superiority, and it may be said that this view of women governs the whole of the parallel play, *The Taming of a Shrew*. But in Shakespeare's play the movement away from Padua to the country house and back again to Padua takes on a new significance so that the view of women changes as the play progresses. Or, to put it more accurately, the chattel speech is never the play's real view of matrimony but is adopted by Petruchio as part of his outrageous mask at the wedding. The audience's realization that Petruchio is game-playing, that he is posing behind the mask of a disorderly male shrew and is having considerable fun exploiting his role, is the key to a romantic reading of the play. Thus Kate is tamed not by Petruchio's whip but by the discovery of her own imagination, for when she learns to recognize the sun for the moon and the moon for the dazzling sun she is discovering the liberating power of laughter and play. In the later festive comedies, the chaos in the middle acts—brought on by the characters' spontaneous love of play and disguise—proves a generative cauldron for magic changes and sudden discoveries of love. If shrewishness is a kind of rigidity, a behavioral pattern locked into closed, predictable responses, then the chaos of play is a liberating force, and Kate's initial bad temper is directly related to her failure to embrace it. In the country-house scenes in the anonymous *A Shrew,* Kate is depersonalized because she is denied any possibilities of play. At one point Ferando offers the famished Kate some pieces of meat on the tip of a dagger in a parody of animal taming. Ferando's purpose is to break Kate's will through hunger and lack of sleep. In Shakespeare's play, however, Petruchio's madcap antics are meant to reduce Kate not so much to hunger as to bewilderment. She is to be immersed in chaos, in that irrational world where we lose our bearings and our old sense of truth, and she is challenged to respond as Christopher Sly does in the Induction by yielding to the confusion, abandoning her old identity in favor of a new one. After a day and night at the country house we learn that Petruchio so

> rails, and swears, and rates, that she, poor soul,
> Knows not which way to stand, to look, to speak,
> And sits as one new-risen from a dream.

In the great comedies to follow, many characters will find themselves, like Kate, "new-risen from a dream," where temporary surrender to the irrational will lead to liberation from former rigidities.

LAUGHTER LEADS TO RENEWAL

Kate's transformation occurs on the road to Padua. All the details of the scene are in the anonymous *A Shrew,* but in that play the incidents are merely a final testing of how efficiently Ferando has broken Kate's will to resist. When Kate reluctantly agrees that the sun is the moon, Ferando replies:

> I am glad *Kate* your stomack is come downe,
> I know it well thou knowest it is the sun,
> But I did trie to see if thou wouldst speake,
> And crosse me now as thou hast donne before,
> And trust me *Kate* hadst thou not named the moone,
> We had gon back againe as sure as death.

There is no laughter on Ferando's part, only a harsh warning that his methods are "as sure as death." Ferando seems as rigid as Kate, and his unyielding authority is nonplayful. In Shakespeare's play, however, Petruchio's method of shrew-taming celebrates life, for Petruchio is playing, and when Kate suddenly joins him, Shakespeare presents her as

cured. Kate's sense of fun throughout the road scene becomes increasingly apparent as she begins to make puns on
"sun" (meaning both the planet and Petruchio, who is "his
mother's son") and as she herself notes the sexual humor in
turning the bewildered old Vincentio into a fresh, budding
virgin. When Petruchio decides to restore Vincentio to himself, Kate, obviously now enjoying her husband's game,
apologizes magnificently:

> Pardon, old father, my mistaking eyes,
> That have been so bedazzled with the sun
> That everything I look on seemeth green.

This emphasis on sunshine and greenness is significant
because the weather during their previous trip from Padua to
the country house was dominated by frost and cold. When
Kate discovers laughter, the weather turns springtime, for
Shakespeare sees in Kate not a taming but a renewal and re-
birth. When she is liberated from shrewishness, she perceives
the world with new eyes and everything "seemeth green."

Kate's transformation, associated as it is with the magical
powers of imagination, is something quite different from the
rough and tumble "taming" she undergoes in *A Shrew*. Her
temporary immersion in chaos is renewing and brings her
in touch with some deeper creative energy. She is neither in-
tellectually nor morally inferior to her husband, and if she is
subordinate to him in the political hierarchy, this difference
does not allow for tyranny but requires instead "honest will"
and "right supremacy." In the final happiness of Kate, we
have thus discovered comic possibilities beyond the primitive limits of farce.

SOME FARCICAL ELEMENTS

And yet the play never breaks completely from farce, and an
emphasis on its romantic elements will be misleading if we
do not see how the romance is at odds with the fabliau. For
example, Petruchio's antics at the country house—his beating of servants, his throwing of food and bedding, his railing
at the tailor—can be accommodated in a romantic reading if
we emphasize, as I have done, the need to create bewilderment and loss of identity in the transforming middle acts of
romantic comedy and if we cite passages such as Curtis's on
Kate's awakening from a dream. These same antics will seem
closer to farce if we cite instead Petruchio's soliloquy beginning "Thus have I politicly begun my reign," in which Petru-

chio compares his taming of Kate to the training of a falcon. This uneasy mixing of romance and farce suggests that Shakespeare's own sense of purpose is unclear, that he is discovering possibilities of one kind of comic structure while working within the demands of another. The coincidence of farce and romance is especially evident during the final wager scene, where the farcical elements prevent the kind of festive conclusion that will mark the later comedies. . . .

[T]he emergence of a humanized heroine demands a comic form completely unlike farce. To emphasize the farcical element in *The Shrew,* therefore, is to neglect the romance inherent in Kate's discovery of laughter, for this is the major difference between Shakespeare's play and earlier versions of shrew-taming. And to insist still on a revisionist conclusion, complete with an untamed Kate and a duped Petruchio, is to show again the alliance of our age with those Renaissance villains who seek liberation from all bondage, especially the bonds of love. It is not Kate's submission to her husband that should make us feel that *The Taming of the Shrew* is more primitive than the later comedies; rather it is the unassimilated elements of farce that continue to depersonalize Kate.

The Taming of the Shrew Satirizes Male Attitudes Toward Women

Coppelia Kahn

Coppelia Kahn, a professor at Brown University, is a noted feminist scholar. By focusing on such topics as gender roles and characters' psychological motivations, Kahn's numerous books and articles have led to new interpretations of Shakespeare's dramas. In this article Kahn argues that males like Christopher Sly and Petruchio, who think they are the masters of submissive wives, are exposed as deluded, and in fact are inferior to women. Kahn points to Petruchio's extreme language and outrageous claims as evidence that Shakespeare is satirizing him. Who could take seriously a male who considers himself the owner of a wife? Who could believe a self-proclaimed knight-errant who pretends to protect his damsel in distress while actually hauling her away from her own wedding feast?

When Kate imitates Petruchio's tone of mastery in her final speech, she is doing so for satiric effect, Kahn claims. Kate is mocking Petruchio's fantasy of male dominance by behaving just as he does. She tells others what to do and think; she uses Petruchio's own preachy tone. Ironically, Kate's actual words of submission also authenticate Petruchio's identity, Kahn explains. Petruchio is dependent on Kate's words to confirm his own identity as a husband and a man. Petruchio's attitudes toward women are satirized, and Kate achieves dominance by mocking Petruchio's attitude.

Though it has long been recognized that Shakespeare gives Kate's "shrewishness" a psychological and moral validity lacking in all literary predecessors, critics still argue that Petruchio's heavy-handed behavior is merely a role briefly

Excerpted from "*The Taming of the Shrew*: Shakespeare's Mirror of Marriage," by Coppelia Kahn, *Modern Language Studies*, vol. 5, 1975. Reprinted by permission of the Northeast Modern Language Association.

assumed for a benign purpose. They claim that he is Kate's savior, the wise man who guides her to a better and truer self, or a clever doctor following homeopathic medicine. They have missed the greatest irony of the play. Unlike other misogynistic shrew literature, this play satirizes not woman herself in the person of the shrew, but *male attitudes toward women.* My purpose is to reveal the ways in which Shakespeare puts these attitudes before us.

SLY IS SATIRIZED

Long before Petruchio enters, we are encouraged to doubt the validity of male supremacy. First of all, the transformation of Christopher Sly from drunken lout to noble lord, a transformation only temporary and skin-deep, suggests that Kate's switch from independence to subjection may also be deceptive, and prepares us for the irony of the dénouement. More pointedly, one of the most alluring perquisites of Sly's new identity is a wife, and his right to domineer over her. As Scene I of the Induction begins, Sly suffers public humiliation at the hands of a woman when the Hostess throws him out of her alehouse for disorderly conduct. After he awakens from his sleep in the second scene, it is the tale of his supposed wife's beauty and Penelope-like devotion and patience that finally tips the balance, convincing him that he really is the aristocrat of the servants' descriptions:

> Am I a lord, and have I such a lady?
> Or do I dream? Or have I dreamed till now?
> I do not sleep: I see, I hear, I speak,
> I smell sweet savors and I feel soft things.
> Upon my life, I am a lord indeed
> And not a tinker nor Christopher Sly.
> Well, bring our lady hither to our sight,
> And once again a pot o' th' smallest ale.

He then glories in demanding and getting his "wife's" obsequious obedience:

> SLY. . . . .
> Where is my wife?
> PAGE. Here, noble lord. What is thy will with her?
> SLY. Are you my wife and will not call me husband?
> My men should call me "lord;" I am your goodman.
> PAGE. My husband and my lord, my lord and husband,
> I am your wife in all obedience.

The humor lies in the fact that Sly's pretensions to authority and grandeur, which he claims only on the basis of sex, not

merit, and indulges specifically with women, are contra-
dicted in his real identity, in which be is a woman's inferior.
Similarly, as I shall argue later, Petruchio seems to find in
Kate the reflection of his own superiority, while we know
that he is fooled by a role she has assumed. . . .

PETRUCHIO BEHAVES LIKE A SHREW

From the moment Petruchio commands his servant "Knock,
I say," he evokes and creates noise and violence. A hubbub of
loud speech, beatings, and quarrelsomeness surrounds him.
"'The swelling Adriatic seas" and "thunder when the clouds
in autumn crack" are a familiar part of his experience, which
he easily masters with his own force of will or physical
strength. Like Adam, he is lord over nature, and his own violence has been well legitimized by society, unlike Kate's,
which has marked her as unnatural and abhorrent. . . .

If Petruchio were female, he would be known as a shrew
and shunned accordingly by men. Behavior desirable in a
male automatically prohibits similar behavior in a female,
for woman must mold herself to be complementary to man,
not competitive with him. Indeed, if manhood is defined and
proven by the ability to dominate, either in battle or in the
household, then a situation which does not allow a man to
dominate is existentially threatening. When Petruchio declares, "I am as peremptory as she proud-minded," he
seems to state that he and his bride-to-be are two of a kind.
But that "kind," bold, independent, self-assertive, must only
be male. Thus his image of himself and Kate as "two raging
fires" ends on a predictable note:

> And where two raging fires meet together
> They do consume the thing that feeds their fury.
> Though little fire grows great with little wind,
> Yet extreme gusts will blow out fire and all.
> So I to her, *and so she yields to me,*
> For I am rough and woo not like a babe.

His force must necessarily triumph over Kate's because he is
male and she is not. Those critics who maintain that his is
acceptable because it has only the limited, immediate purpose of making Kate reject an "unbecoming" mode of behavior miss the real point of the taming. The overt force
Petruchio wields over Kate by marrying her against her will
in the first place, and then by denying her every wish and
comfort, stamping, shouting, reducing her to exhaustion,

etc., is but a farcical representation of the psychological realities of marriage in Elizabethan England, in which the
husband's will constantly, silently, and invisibly, through
custom and conformity, suppressed the wife's.

PETRUCHIO'S STRATEGY FOR MASTERY

At the wedding in Act III, scene 1, Petruchio's behavior trav-
esties the decorum, ceremony and piety which all those present feel ought to accompany a marriage. It is calculated to
deprive Kate of the opportunity to enjoy the bride's sense of
triumph, of being the center of admiration and interest; to
humiliate her in public; to throw her off her guard by convincing her he is mad; and to show her that now nothing can
happen unless and until her husband pleases. The final effect of the wedding scene, however, is less comical than the
rhetorically delightful accounts of Petruchio's of stage antics.
When all the trappings are stripped away (and they are, by
his design), the groom is simply completing the legal
arrangements whereby he acquires Kate as he would ac-
quire a piece of property. When be declares he'll "seal the
title with a lovely kiss," he refers not just to Kate's new title
as his wife, but also to the title-deed which, sealed with wax,
passed to the purchaser in a property transaction. Tranio remarks of Petruchio, "He hath some meaning in his mad attire," and he is right. When Petruchio says "To me she's married, not unto my clothes," he assumes a lofty morality,
implying that he offers Kate real love, not just its worldly
show. This moralistic pose becomes an important part of his
strategy in Act IV when he claims to do nothing that isn't for
Kate's "good." But in the brutally plain statement he delivers
at the conclusion of the wedding scene, he momentarily
drops this pose:

> She is my goods, my chattels; she is my house,
> My household stuff, my field, my barn,
> My horse, my ox, my ass, my anything.

His role as property-owner is the model for his role as husband; Kate, for him, is a thing. Or at least she will become a
thing when he has wrenched unquestioning obedience from
her, when she no longer has mind or will of her own. It is
impossible that Shakespeare meant us to accept Petruchio's
speech uncritically: it is the most shamelessly blunt statement of the relationship between men, women, and property
to be found in the literature of this period. After the simple

declarative statements of possession, quoted above, which deny humanity to Kate, the speech shifts to chivalric challenges of imaginary "thieves" who would snatch her away. Is she goods, in the following lines, or a medieval damsel?

> ... Touch her whoever dare,
> I'll bring mine action on the proudest he
> That stops my way in Padua. Grumio,
> Draw forth thy weapon, we are beset with thieves.
> Rescue thy mistress, if thou be a man.

The point is that Petruchio wants to think of her in both kinds of terms. The speech concludes grandly with the metamorphosis of Petruchio, into a knight-errant:

> Fear not, sweet wench; they shall not touch thee, Kate.
> I'll buckler thee against a million.

The modulation of simple ownership into spurious chivalry reveals the speaker's buried awareness that be cheapens himself by being merely Kate's proprietor; he must transform the role into something nobler.

Petruchio's thundering oaths and physical brutality reach a crescendo at his country house in Act IV, when he beats his servants, throws food and dishes on the floor, stomps, roars and bullies. These actions are directed not against his bride but at his servants, again in the name of chivalry out of a fastidious devotion to his bride's supposed comfort. But his stance is rooted realistically in his status as lord of a manor and master of a household which is not Kate's but his. He ordered her wedding clothes, chose their style and paid for them. Kate wears them not at her pleasure but at his, as Grumio's jest succinctly indicates:

> PETRUCHIO. Well, sir, in brief, the gown is not for me.
> GRUMIO.   You are i' th' right, sir; 'tis for my mistress.

In the famous soliloquy which opens "Thus have I politicly begun my reign," Petruchio reduces Kate to an animal capable of learning only through deprivation of food and rest, devoid of all sensitivity save the physical. The animal metaphor shocks us and I would suggest was meant to shock Shakespeare's audience, despite their respect for falconry as an art and that reverence for the great chain of being emphasized by E.M.W. Tillyard. I suppose Kate is actually being elevated in this speech, in view of previous references to her as her husband's horse, ox, and ass, for a falcon was the appurtenance of a nobleman, and a valued animal. But the blandness of Petruchio's confidential tone, the sweep of his easy assumption that Kate is not merely an animal, but *his* animal, who lives or dies at his command—has a dramatic irony similar to that of his exit speech in the wedding scene. Both utterances unashamedly present the status of woman in marriage as degrading in the extreme, plainly declaring her a sub-human being who exists solely for the purposes of her husband. Yet both offer this vision of the wife as chattel or animal in a lordly, self-confident tone. Urbanity is super-imposed on outrage, for our critical scrutiny.

Shakespeare does not rest with showing that male su-premacy in marriage denies woman's humanity. In the most brilliant comic scene of the play (IV.5), he goes on to demon-strate how it defies reason. Petruchio demands that Kate agree that the sun is the moon in order to force a final show-down. Having exhausted and humiliated her to the limit of his invention, be now wants her to know that he would go to any extreme to get the obedience he craves. Shakespeare im-plies here that male supremacy is ultimately based on such absurdities, for it insists that whatever a man says is right be-cause he is a man, even if he happens to be wrong. In a male-supremacist utopia, masculinity might be identical with ab-solute truth, but in life the two coincide only intermittently.

KATE APPEARS TO SUBMIT

Why does Kate submit to her husband's unreason? Or why does she *appear* to do so, and on what terms? On the most pragmatic level, she follows Hortensio's advice to "Say as he says or we shall never go" only in order to achieve her im-mediate and most pressing needs: a bed, a dinner, some peace and quiet. Shakespeare never lets us think that she be-lieves it right, either morally or logically, to submit her judg-ment and the evidence of her senses to Petruchio's rule. In fact, the language of her capitulation makes it clear that she thinks him mad:

> Forward, I pray, since we have come so far,
> And be it moon or sun or what you please.
> *And if you please to call it a rush-candle,*
> Henceforth I vow it shall be so for me.
>
> .   .   .   .
>
> But sun it is not when you say it is not,
> *And the moon changes even as your mind.*

At this point, Hortensio concedes Petruchio's victory and applauds it; Petruchio henceforth behaves and speaks as though he has indeed tamed Kate. However, we must assume that since he previously donned the mask of the ardent lover, professing rapture at Kate's rudeness, he can see that she is doing the same thing here. At their first meeting he turned the tables on her, praising her for mildness and modesty after she gave insults and even injury. Now she pays him back, suddenly overturning his expectations and moreover mocking them at the same time. But he is not fooled, and can take that mockery as the cue for compromise. It reassures him that she will give him obedience if that is what he must have, but it also warns him that she, in turn, must retain her intellectual freedom.

The scene then proceeds on this basis, each character accepting the other's assumed role. Kate responds to Petruchio's outrageous claim that the wrinkled Vincentio is a fair young maiden by pretending so wholeheartedly to accept it that we know she can't be in earnest. She embroiders the fantasy in an exuberant declamatory style more appropriate to tragedy than comedy:

> Young budding virgin, fair and fresh and sweet,
> Whither away, or where is thy abode?
> Happy the parents of so fair a child!
> Happier the man whom favorable stars
> Allots thee for his lovely bedfellow!

Her rhetoric expresses her realization that the power struggle she had entered into on Petruchio's terms is absurd. It also signals her emancipation from that struggle, in the terms she declared earlier: ". . . I will be free / Even to the uttermost, as I please, in words."

Of course, a freedom that exists only in words is ultimately as limited as Petruchio's mastery. Though Kate is clever enough to use his verbal strategies against him, she is trapped in her own cleverness. Her only way of maintaining her inner freedom is by outwardly denying it, which thrusts her into a schizoid existence. . . .

THE IRONIC FINAL SCENE

In the last scene, Shakespeare finally allows Petruchio that lordship over Kate, and superiority to other husbands, for which he has striven so mightily. He just makes it clear to us, through the contextual irony of Kate's last speech, that her husband is deluded. As a contest between males in which woman is the prize, the closing scene is analogous to the entire play. It was partly Petruchio's desire to show his peers that he was more of a man than they which spurred him to take on the shrew in the first place. Gremio refers to him as a Hercules and compares the subduing of Kate to a "labor . . . more than Alcides' twelve." Hortensio longs but fails to emulate his friend's supposed success in taming. Lucentio, winner in the other wooing context, fails in the final test of marital authority. Petruchio stands alone in the last scene, the center of male admiration.

As critics have noted, the wager scene is punctuated by reversals: quiet Bianca talks back and shrewish Kate seems to become an obedient wife. In a further reversal, however, she steals the scene from her husband, who has held the stage throughout the play, and reveals that he has failed to tame her in the sense he set out to. He has gained her outward compliance in the form of a public display, while her spirit remains mischievously free. Though she pretends to speak earnestly on behalf of her own inferiority, she actually treats us to a pompous, wordy, holier-than-thou sermon which delicately mocks the sermons her husband has delivered to her and about her. It is significant that Kate's speech is both her longest utterance and the longest in the play. Previously, Petruchio dominated the play verbally, and his longest speech totalled twenty-four lines, while Kate's came to fifteen. Moreover, everything Kate said was a protest against her situation or those who put her in it, and as such was deemed unwomanly, or shrewish. Petruchio's impressive rhetoric, on the other hand, asserted his masculinity in the form of command over women and servants and of moral authority. Now Kate apes this verbal dominance and moralistic stance for satirical effect.

In content, the speech is thoroughly orthodox. Its sentiments can be found in a dozen treatises on marriage written in the sixteenth century. The arguments that a woman's beauty is her greatest asset and depends on her amiability; that her obedience is a debt rendered in return for financial support; that the household is a hierarchy like the state, with husband as lord and wife as subject; that the female's physical delicacy fits her only for meekness—all were the platitudes of male dominance. Kate offers them with complete seriousness, straightforwardly except for a few verbal ironies, such as the reminder of her husband's rhetorical patterns in "thy lord, thy life, thy keeper, / Thy bead, thy sovereign," which echoes his "my goods, my chattels; . . . my house, / My household stuff, my field, my barn / my horse, my ox, my ass, my anything." The grave moral tone of the speech, as I have noted, comes from Petruchio also, but its irony emanates primarily from the dramatic context. First, it follows upon and resembles Kate's rhetorical performance on the road back to Padua. It is a response to her husband's demand that she demonstrate her obedience before others, as she did then before Hortensio, and as such it exceeds expectations once more. It fairly shouts obedience, when a gentle murmur would suffice. Having heard her address Vincentio as "Young, budding virgin," we know what she is up to in this instance. Second, though the speech pleads subordination, as a speech—a lengthy, ambitious verbal performance before an audience—it allows the speaker to dominate that audience. Though Kate purports to speak as a woman to women, she assumes the role of a preacher whose authority and wisdom are, in the terms of the play, thoroughly masculine. Third, the speech sets the seal on a complete reversal of character, a push-button change from rebel to conformist which is, I have argued, part of the mechanism of farce. Here as elsewhere in the play, farce has two purposes: it completes the fantasy of male dominance, but also mocks it as mere fantasy. Kate's quick transformation perfectly fulfills Petruchio's wishes, but is transparently false to human nature. Towards the end of her lecture, Kate hints that she is dissembling in the line "That seeming to be most which we indeed least are." Though she seems to be the most vocal apologist for male dominance, she is indeed its ablest critic.

PETRUCHIO'S FANTASY IS MOCKED

On one level, the dénouement is the perfect climax of a masculine fantasy, for as Kate concludes she prepares to place her hand beneath her husband's foot, an emblem-book symbol of wifely obedience. On a deeper level as I have tried to show, her words speak louder than her actions, and mock that fantasy. But on the deepest level, because the play depicts its heroine as outwardly compliant but inwardly independent, it represents possibly the most cherished male fantasy of all—that woman remain *un*tamed, even in her subjection. Does Petruchio know he's been taken? Quite probably, since he himself has played the game of saying-the-thing-which-is-not. Would he enjoy being married to a woman as dull and proper as the Kate who delivers that marriage sermon? From all indications, no. Then can we conclude that Petruchio no less than Kate knowingly plays a false role in this marriage, the role of victorious tamer and complacent master? I think we can, but what does this tell us about him and about men in general?

It is Kate's submission to him which makes Petruchio a man, finally and indisputably. This is the action toward which the whole plot drives, and if we consider its significance for Petruchio and his fellows we realize that the myth of feminine weakness, which prescribes that women ought to or must inevitably submit to man's superior authority, masks a contrary myth: that only a woman has the power to authenticate a man, by acknowledging him *her* master. Petruchio's mind may change even as the moon, but what is important is that Kate confirm those changes; moreover, that she do so willingly and consciously. Such voluntary surrender is, paradoxically, part of the myth of female power, which assigns to woman the crucial responsibility for creating a mature and socially respectable man. In *The Taming of the Shrew,* Shakespeare reveals the dependency which underlies mastery, the strength behind submission. Truly, Petruchio is wedded to his Kate.

Petruchio's Conquest of Kate Is a Mating Dance

Michael West

University of Pittsburgh professor Michael West claims that critics and readers of *The Taming of the Shrew* focus on the issue of women's rights in the play, while live audiences respond with delight to the sexual rites presented on the stage. West notices the many references to dancing in the play, then suggests that Petruchio's strutting and biceps-flexing resemble a mating dance. West compares Petruchio's pursuit of Kate to any healthy male animal's pursuit of a healthy female. Onstage Petruchio's physical exuberance and verbal strutting are as effective as a peacock's mating dance. The taming is really no more than teasing that tantalizes Kate, West asserts. Kate's final speech, in West's estimation, is her way of saying yes to the demands and joys of sex. The animal imagery in the play bothers some readers, but West argues that it is perfectly appropriate for a play about the consummation of a marriage.

Upon his first appearance Petruchio, in a nodal [central] image, describes his wanderings to Hortensio: "I have thrust myself into this maze, / Haply to wive and thrive as best I may." Though not usually so glossed, *maze* probably refers to the Elizabethan dance pattern; for when Hortensio goes on to mention a rich heiress, Petruchio promptly professes his intention to marry her, "As wealth is burden of my wooing dance." Hortensio's reply may even faintly echo this governing metaphor: "Petruchio, since we are stepped thus far in, / I will continue." The initial scene has dramatized Kate as threatened by spinsterhood: "'Mates,' maid, how mean you that? No mates for you / Unless you were of gentler, milder mold." Throughout the play, Petruchio's brusque pur-

Excerpted from "The Folk Background of Petruchio's Wooing Dance: Male Supremacy in *The Taming of the Shrew*," by Michael West, *Shakespeare Studies*, vol. 7, 1974. Reprinted by permission of the University of South Carolina Press.

suit of her is to be viewed as a kind of mating dance with a spirited partner whose sexual appeal he frankly acknowledges: "Now, by the world, it is a lusty wench." One critic [M.C. Bradbrook] has casually but aptly noted that "his demonstrations of physical exuberance, wit and bawdry are provocative courting plumage." A sixteenth-century theorist like Thoinot Arbeau could justify dancing as necessary to preserve a hierarchical social order, functioning as a means whereby lovers explored each other's health and strength. Thus the elaborately patterned verbal strutting of Petruchio's first conversation with Kate leads to his command "O, let me see thee walk. Thou dost not halt" and his praise for her "princely gait," while the lack of a bridegroom makes Kate complain bitterly that she "must dance barefoot" on her sister's wedding day. As Renaissance theologians disapprovingly stressed, weddings were often distinguished by dancing of an exuberant and cheerful sensuality. . . .

ANIMAL IMAGERY IS APPROPRIATE

If Petruchio's conquest of Kate is a kind of mating dance with appropriate strutting and biceps-flexing, she in turn is a healthy female animal who wants a male strong enough to protect her, deflower her, and sire vigorous offspring. Petruchio's elemental force differentiates him from the numerous old pantaloons who people the comic world of the play, especially the Bianca plot. Alexander Barclay's *Mirror of Good Maners* was characteristic of the Renaissance in pinpointing where the inadequacy of an aging suitor was revealed: "Not well presentith he the wower in a daunce, / But very ill he playeth the volage amorous / Which fetered in a gine woulde gambalde leape & praunce, / Attached to a chayne of linkes ponderous." The animal imagery in which the play abounds is a prime reason for its disfavor with the critics, who find such terms degrading to Kate and to the concept of matrimony. True, Petruchio undertakes to "woo this wildcat" and punningly vows "to tame you, Kate, / And bring you from a wild Kate to a Kate / Comfortable as other household Kates." Likewise, there is the nodal metaphor of hawk taming, and at the end he wagers on her obedience as on his horse or his hound. But these images are less the mark of the master than his tribute to the animal spirits that they both share. He is perfectly willing to style himself "a combless cock, so Kate will be my hen." If she can be compared to the jennet in *Venus and Adonis,* inwardly eager but coyly standoffish, Petruchio's behavior recalls the stallion's in that poem: "Anon he rears upright, curvets, and leaps, / As who should say, 'Lo, thus my strength is tried, / And this I do to captivate the eye / Of the fair breeder that is standing by.'" Shakespeare's easy acceptance of the facts learned in War-wickshire barnyards, his evident sympathy for all animal life, should forestall any critical squeamishness on our part. His Elizabethan audience, after all, could cheerfully look for guidance to a marriage manual like Pierre Viret's *The Schoole of Beastes, intituled, the good Housholder* (London, 1585), where behavior proper to husbands and wives is approvingly illustrated with a host of euphuistic comparisons drawn exclusively from the animal kingdom. We should remember that when Hamlet eulogizes man as angelic in action and godlike in apprehension, he is at the same time perfectly capable of viewing him as "the paragon of animals.". . .

Far from degrading Petruchio and Kate, then, animal imagery is profoundly appropriate for a play the major action of which takes place on a honeymoon. Somehow, most criticism has contrived to ignore the fact that Kate's handling by her husband represents among other things a spirited young creature's sexual initiation by a handsomely qualified male animal. However, in this connection we must note that Shakespeare is very careful not to have Petruchio wrest conjugal rights from an unwilling bride, as one suspects the authors of some of the analogues would cheerfully have permitted. As his punning with her name suggests Petruchio regards his "super-dainty Kate" as a choice piece, a sensual morsel, "for dainties are all cates." Yet Kate is scarcely diminished through being eyed frankly as a sexual object, for a similar appetite is presumed to underlie her interest in him. Thus in the play's poetic pattern the starvation training that Petruchio inflicts upon her functions as a theatrical symbol for appetite denied. Instead of raping his bride, Petruchio teases her by deliberately postponing the consummation of their marriage. Their first night at their new home finds him, as Curtis informs us, "in her chamber, making a sermon of continency to her," to her stunned amazement. Tantalized with the possibility of a satisfied appetite, sleep, and the wifely garb emblematic of full-blown womanliness, Kate must learn to behave in a way that will allow the sexual act to take place properly, *ille supra, illa subter* [he above, she below]. Indeed, there is a profound sense that only with this act is the marriage fully valid.

KATE SAYS "YES"

From this felt necessity the climax of the play derives its poetic force. Kate's long speech of feminine submission is not primarily ironic—a morally obnoxious notion that would forbid us to admire domination based on honest force while sanctioning manipulation based on guile. On the other hand, her speech is not primarily a recipe for the male's domestic and social tyranny. Although the overt terms are domestic and social, and as such can be paralleled by similar Elizabethan pronouncements, within the poetic pattern of the play the speech functions mainly as a token of Kate's acquiescence to the demands and joys of sex. Her willing capitulation thus fulfills a rhythm fundamental to much comic drama. Petruchio can scarcely be expected to tup Kate onstage; Elizabethan censorship would not have tolerated an *Oh Calcutta*. But such explicitness was scarcely necessary for the men and women in Shakespeare's audience. They could be relied upon to interpret Kate's speech of submission with imaginative responsibility. They knew what to make of a tableau where she kneels to embrace Petruchio's foot and then both promptly and explicitly hustle offstage to bed. With a reigning queen on the throne, they were in no danger of taking literally Kate's extravagant verbal endorsement of male superiority, any more than one can imagine the grocer's wife in Beaumont's *Knight of the Burning Pestle* espousing such an attitude toward her husband. Indeed, to thwart any misconception on this point Shakespeare begins with Christopher Sly's bumbling, graphically illustrating the difficulty of translating what is essentially a poetic vision of male sexual supremacy into everyday reality.

SEXUAL RITES, NOT WOMEN'S RIGHTS

In sum, criticism has generally misconstrued the issue of the play as women's rights, whereas what the audience delightedly responds to are sexual rites. When Shaw fumed that no man of decency could witness the play's end in the company of a lady without feeling embarrassment, he was preoccupied with women's suffrage when he should have been thinking of the sundry damsels whose sexual conquest he devoted himself to with frank relish. While he stayed up to write his review, one suspects that some of the couples in that turn-of-the-century audience had found a better way of reconciling their differences, at least temporarily. Petruchio and Kate's relationship is less a model for the domestic and social subjugation of women than a theatrical metaphor for a kind of male dominance often expressed in erotic contexts and not necessarily elsewhere. Indeed, properly understood, the play's ideals may not be so hostile to those of a modern feminist. Far from idealizing the wishy-washy stereotypically feminine subservience of a Bianca, Shakespeare's play is suffused with the sense that spirited and independent women like Kate make not only the best bedmates and the best helpmeets, but are simply the most fun to be with as people. In this it is of a piece with the later comedies. Shakespeare would probably have agreed with Sir John Davies in viewing not only courtship but marriage itself as a dance:

> What if by often enterchange of place
> Sometime the woman gets the vpper hand?
> That is but done for more delightful grace,
> For on that part shee doth not euer stand;
> But, as the measure's law doth her command,
> Shee wheeles about, and ere the daunce doth end,
> Into her former place shee doth transcend.

One may reasonably assume that Petruchio and Kate look forward to a flexible marriage in which both partners are sufficiently secure about their sexual roles to have mastered the "delightful grace" of not being confined to them.

Domestic Violence in *The Taming of the Shrew*

Emily Detmer

Emily Detmer, assistant professor of English at Millikin University in Illinois, makes use of recent psychological research on controlling and abusive behavior to interpret Petruchio's taming of Kate. She argues that Petruchio's methods, though not physically violent, are nevertheless coercive and controlling. In this article Detmer first describes the Stockholm syndrome, a psychological phenomenon where victims actually bond and sympathize with their abusers. She then compares Petruchio's methods with those used by hostage-holders and domestic abusers to elicit cooperation. Detmer explains that Petruchio uses threats, isolates Kate in his country house, and treats her with alternating kindness and aggression. His purpose, like that of actual domestic abusers, is to control her thoughts and actions through fear and intimidation. Petruchio might have been praised in the sixteenth century for not beating his wife into submission, but his coercive methods for achieving domestic harmony would be called emotional abuse by many feminist activists today, Detmer concludes.

For the past twenty-five years battered women and human-rights activists have worked together to reformulate what constitutes domestic violence; they identify physical violence as only one of many tactics abusers use to control and subordinate their victims. From this perspective domestic violence is any act of coercion that aims to nullify a person's will or desire in order for the abuser to gain dominance. Instead of limiting the definition of domestic violence to a certain kind of behavior, such as physical battery, this model

Excerpted from "Civilizing Subordination: Domestic Violence and *The Taming of the Shrew*," by Emily Detmer, *Shakespeare Quarterly*, vol. 48, no. 3, 1997. Reprinted by permission of the Associated University Presses.

places controlling behavior on a continuum of oppression. Many feminist activists insist that domestic violence is not exclusively defined as hitting a woman/wife; it encompasses a range of behaviors that includes intimidation, isolation, threats, emotional abuse, economic manipulation, and sexual assault. Ironically, the early modern reform movement, with its emphasis on replacing beating with other controlling behaviors, put in place the very model that many twentieth-century feminists are working to dismantle.

Petruchio's methods of taming Kate, which can be read as participating in the early modern wife-beating reform movement, can also be read as abusive through the lens of twentieth-century feminist work on domestic violence. The cultural meaning of Petruchio's violence is not the same now as it was in its original context. But when we "historicize" the play—for ourselves or our students—we should not only account for sixteenth- and seventeenth-century notions of domestic violence; we need to consider twentieth-century notions of violence as well. For the remainder of this essay, I will explore Petruchio's method not in relation to early modern reforms but in terms of twentieth-century feminist notions of domestic violence and what is known as the Stockholm syndrome in particular. My intention is neither to find nor to confirm a diagnosis of abuse; Petruchio and Kate are not real people, after all. Yet the Stockholm syndrome provides a useful contrast to the falcon-training model so often used to understand the taming. More importantly, it provides a lens through which to scrutinize a kind of interpersonal violence within heterosexual relations which the play's comedy seeks to romanticize. . . .

THE STOCKHOLM SYNDROME

The controlling and coercive methods Petruchio uses to tame Kate are similar to the actions found in one particular kind of domestic-violence dynamic, known as the Stockholm syndrome. The name of this syndrome refers to a 1973 bank-robbery/hostage situation in which the hostages bonded with their captors. The syndrome explains why hostages appear to submit to rather than resist their captors; it describes the paradoxical bond, even affection, that arises in many hostage situations. While the Stockholm syndrome was originally identified in relation to the extraordinary event of hostage-taking, it evolved into a diagnostic tool to

explain the more frequent situation of the abusive household. Feminist sociologists found a correlation in the survival behaviors of both hostages and victims of domestic violence. Both the abuser and the hostage-taker assert
complete control over the victim's thoughts and actions
through fear and intimidation. The Stockholm syndrome occurs when: 1) a person threatens another's survival and is
perceived by the other as able and willing to carry out
his/her threat; 2) the threatening person shows the other
kindness; 3) the victim is unable to escape from the threatening person; and 4) the victim is isolated from outsiders.

Shakespeare's Petruchio is, in terms of Stockholm-syn-
drome categories, the quintessential abuser: he isolates Kate
from those who could intervene on her behalf, and he
threatens her survival "in the name of perfect love." Kate,
like other hostages, finds that the key to survival will be to
"actively develop strategies for staying alive." In Kate's situation these strategies entail denying her sense of reality and
speaking as if she sees the world through Petruchio's eyes.

DESIRE FOR CONTROL

At the heart of violent and coercive behavior is the desire for
control. Throughout the play, Petruchio makes clear that he
tames Kate in order to make her "conformable;" he wants total control over her thoughts and actions, no matter how
trivial. Even before they meet, Petruchio plans to interpret
the meanings of her words contrary to her intent, thereby
staking a claim over her language. Petruchio outlines his
method of "woo[ing] contradiction;" he will misread the
meaning of either her words or her silence:

> Say she be mute and will not speak
> Then I'll commend her volubility
> And say she uttereth piercing eloquence.
> If she do bid me pack, I'll give her thanks;
> As though she bid me stay by her a week.
> If she deny to wed, I'll crave the day
> When I shall ask the banns, and when be married.

Simply thus contradicting her meaning, however, might
leave her confused but not under his control. He therefore issues his first threat at their initial meeting. Although they
toss words to each other in a seemingly playful way, by the
end of the scene, Petruchio stops playing and lays down his
intent in a menacing way: "And will you, nil you, I will

marry you." Here Petruchio establishes that, while their mutual wordplay has been fun, he will take her as his wife with
or without her consent. When their marriage proves how little her consent matters, Petruchio's power over her language
and her person is secured.

THREATS

Rather than beat Kate into submission, he threatens her in a
manner that recalls the Stockholm syndrome, coercing her
into internalizing his wishes if she is to eat or sleep or escape
isolation: "She ate no meat today, nor none shall eat; / Last
night she slept not, nor tonight she shall not." Depriving her
of both food and sleep will make her weak and materially
dependent on him. Like the method used to train a falcon, he
tells the audience, his method to "man" his "haggard" will
make her "stoop" and "make her come and know her
keeper's call." While these are particularly egregious exam-
ples, the subtle coercions of the Stockholm syndrome appear
throughout the play.

Petruchio demonstrates to Kate that he can carry out even
the most outrageous threats. He aggressively pursues the
"clapped up" wedding but then does not come at the ap-
pointed time. Although she is marrying him "against her
heart," Kate's status now depends on his arrival. Being left
standing at the altar is here a kind of violence—even her father pities Kate by saying the "*injury* would vex a saint"—
and Petruchio delays long enough to make his arrival seem
like a special kindness. When he does finally appear, he is
dressed in ridiculous garb described as "an eyesore" and a
"shame to [his] estate." When the wedding guests express
outrage, Petruchio claims, "To me she's married, not unto
my clothes." While this scene is often regarded as evidence
that Petruchio is a "madcap" fool, it also demonstrates his
power to do as he pleases. Tranio alerts the audience to the
possibility that Petruchio's choice of "unreverent robes" is a
strategy ("He hath some meaning in his mad attire") but
concludes that the best the men of Padua can hope for is to
"persuade" him to change his clothing before going into
church. Though everyone onstage is aghast at Petruchio's
behavior, none dares interfere. According to Gremio's re-
port, no one intervenes in Petruchio's aggression during the
wedding either. As Kate "trembled and shook," Petruchio
"stamped and swore" while striking a priest, throwing wine-

soaked cake in the sexton's face, and acting as if he were "carousing with his mates." Although Gremio feels shame at the unseemly behavior ("And I, seeing this, came thence for very shame"), neither he nor anyone else stops it. Obviously this community will not discipline a head of household. This sets up Petruchio's behavior as threatening and aggressive, even to the bystanders, as well as establishing that in this early modern marriage a husband can carry out any threat against his wife.

ALTERNATING KINDNESS AND AGGRESSION

Although none of the men challenge his behavior, Kate stands up to him. She tries several strategies to negotiate a more acceptable response. Trying to persuade him to stay for the customary wedding feast, she first entreats Petruchio through an exchange of affection: "Now, if you love me, stay." But once this fails, she reverts to an earlier strategy of anger and frank speech: "Gentlemen, forward to the bridal dinner. / I see a woman may be made a fool / If she had not a spirit to resist." Petruchio establishes his dominance by verbally confirming her command while physically preventing her words from achieving their intent. Urging the others to feast without her because "she must with me. . . . I will be master of what is mine own," he then transforms his role as "master" into a gesture of kindly protection. Acting as if the wedding guests intend to abduct Kate ("we are beset with thieves"), he draws his sword and threatens her family. While refusing Kate her wedding feast, a simple pleasure she regards as her due, he converts her forced removal into a rescue: "Fear not, sweet wench, they shall not touch thee, Kate." Petruchio's mock rescue combines kindness with aggression and confuses Kate's sense of his domination. Kate will later complain that Petruchio "rails and swears and raves" all through their wedding night, and yet he calls it love. When they have arrived at Petruchio's own residence, he orders a dress and cap made for Kate but then refuses to allow her to accept them: "When you are gentle you shall have one too, / And not till then." He repeatedly alternates kindness with aggression, and that which at first appears an act of kindness and provision becomes another chance to deprive her and thus confirms his control of her environment. As researchers have found, in a situation that is totally violent, victims soon give up trying to please. When, however, abusers show kindness and concern for their victims, it creates an emotional bond; abusers "ease the emotional distress they have created and . . . set the stage for emotional dependency." Alternating coercive threats and kindness sets up a situation where victims *actively* look for ways to please rather than upset their captors.

ISOLATION

A key factor in the development of the syndrome is isolation and the inability to escape. When Kate is taken to Petruchio's house, where even the servants refuse to sneak her food, she is isolated from anyone who can help her. Her father, traditionally the person who would protect her, has established that he wishes to be rid of her; she feels as if she has been put up for sale; "is it your will / To make a stale of me?" Even though Baptista has said "love is all," no one seems to care whether Kate consents to the marriage or not. At first Gremio notices that her words are words of protest: "Hark, Petruchio, she says she'll see thee hanged first." But Tranio silences him, pointing out that paying attention to her wishes will not help their mutual cause. Then Petruchio intervenes and undermines any further verbal refusal on her part by saying that he and she have made a "bargain" between them that "she will still be cursed" in public. Since all the men around her conspire to ignore the fact that she does not consent to a marriage to Petruchio, Kate has little hope that they will later intervene on her behalf.

The scenes that take place in Petruchio's house in Act 4 best exemplify the Stockholm syndrome. Some may question whether Kate's "survival" was ever really at stake, but from Kate's point of view, there is no way to know how long this "brawling" might last; she states explicitly her fear that it may lead to a "deadly sickness or else present death." Food and sleep have been withheld from her for no apparent reason. While the threat to Kate's survival is most keen at this point, Petruchio's repeated use of violence against subordinates also contributes to a state in which she fears for her life, another of the key elements of the syndrome.

BONDING WITH THE ABUSER

Because Kate is completely isolated and convinced that Petruchio could carry out any of his threats, she must bond with her abuser in order to survive. Dee Graham and Edna

Rawlings argue that the Stockholm syndrome in abused women follows this pattern:

> The abuser traumatizes the victim (who cannot escape) with threat to survival. The traumatized victim needs nurturance and protection. Being isolated from outsiders, the victim must turn to the abuser for nurturance and protection, as she denies her rage. If the abuser shows the victim some small kindness, the victim bonds to the positive side of abuse. . . . The victim works to see the world from the abuser's perspective so that she will know what will keep the abuser happy.

Petruchio's and Kate's actions at his house and on the road back to Padua match this description. Kate learns that to survive she must see (or at least claim to see) the world from his perspective, just as she learns to bond with this side of his abuse.

It takes repeated effort for Kate before she can learn to "deny her rage." She struggles against Petruchio's systematic destruction of her will by demanding to be heard:

> My tongue will tell the anger of my heart,
> Or else my heart concealing it will break,
> And rather than it shall, I will be free
> Even to the uttermost, as I please, in words.

This eloquent speech about her vital need to speak is the last one the audience hears in which Kate has a substantial sense of self and autonomy. Petruchio denies her language (and her sense of self) by pretending to hear in her words merely a comment on a cap: "Why, thou say's true, it is a paltry cap. . . . I love thee well in that thou lik'st it not." Again combining kindness with aggression, he performs his absolute power and control over her without touching her. He tests her tendency "to cross" him until she submits, that is, until she "incorporates the world view of the aggressor."

Petruchio offers her a bit of kindness and an escape from her isolation with a visit to her father's house. But he threatens to retract the offer if she does not second his perverse reading of time and space. When he asserts that the present time is seven, Kate corrects him. He demands:

> It shall be seven ere I go to horse.
> Look what I speak, or do, or think to do,
> You are still crossing it. Sirs, let 't alone,
> I will not go today, and ere I go,
> It shall be what o'clock I say it is.

Petruchio has the power to say what time it is against any authority (such as the sun). What is at stake is Kate's willingness to "cross" him. His assertion must be sovereign, even if it is absurd or contrary to everything Kate knows. His goal is complete power and control over her thoughts and actions. In one of the most widely discussed scenes of the play, Hortensio urges Kate to speak against her own knowledge: "Say as he says, or we shall never go." Petruchio again offers his test, "I say it is the moon that shines so bright," and Kate responds out of her own knowledge: "I know it is the sun that shines so bright." But when Petruchio threatens to take her back to the isolation of his home, Kate begins to "see" the world—that is, the sun and the moon—through Petruchio's eyes. She shifts her strategies and, when he repeats his "I say it is the moon," responds as he wished all along: "I know it is the moon." Her language of "know[ing]" here underscores Petruchio's gesture as an effort to change her source of knowledge.

From Petruchio's point of view, Kate's resistance has been about crossing him: "Ever more crossed and crossed, nothing but crossed." When she finally goes along with Petruchio's claims about the sun and the moon and later about Vincentio, Hortensio announces that the war is over. Defeated, Kate has surrendered herself as hostage: "The field is won." While the field is not bloody and her body is not black and blue, the process that Kate has undergone is nonetheless abusive because it signifies Petruchio's domination over her speech and actions.

A COERCED HARMONY

A model of domestic violence that includes tactics other than physical violence gives readers a way in which to understand Kate's romanticized surrender at the end of the play as something other than consensual, as, in fact, a typical response to abuse. Although Kate's final speech is her longest, it does not necessarily reflect her own thoughts, desires, and wishes. Like a victim of the Stockholm syndrome, she denies her own feelings in order to bond with her abuser. Her surrender and obedience signify her emotional bondage as a survival strategy; she aims to please because her life depends on it. Knowing how the Stockholm syndrome works can help us to see that whatever "subjectivity" might be achieved is created out of domination and a coercive bonding.

The heterosexual romance plot of the play encourages readers to see this bonding as "love" and to disregard the violence of taming. Even though the play's spectators witness a husband attaining a coercive emotional bond with his wife through systematic abuse, the violence is easily discounted because there are no physical blows. While we have little sympathy with women who stay with (and continue to "love") a physically abusive husband, we still seem to follow the model put forth in the play. If the victim's injuries are physical, our culture doesn't see the accompanying coercive bonds as romantic; if the injuries are invisible, our culture, like the early modern, tolerates them. *The Taming of the Shrew* participates in a cultural tradition that accepts coercive bonding and oppression as long as they are free of physical violence. . . .

DIFFERENT NOTIONS OF KINDNESS

When Petruchio boasts that his method "is a way to kill a wife with kindness," he relies on several notions of "kindness." At one level, he means that his haggard-manning method is "kind" in comparison with the beating she might have experienced. Another meaning of "kindness" plays on giving back the same "kind" of shrewishness Kate embodies; they are two of a kind, as several critics have argued. But a third element of "kindness" emerges in the combined threat to "kill" while simultaneously acting "kind." As the Stockholm syndrome demonstrates, hostages bond with their captors when, at the same time their lives are threatened, they are shown some gestures of kindness.

Just as the meaning of Petruchio's "kindness" is multiple, domestic violence can be defined in more than one way. If a culture identifies violence by the level of brutality and physical injury, then Petruchio provides a useful method of gaining the wifely subordination that early modern men considered natural and right, without resorting to wife-beating. Under the guise of civility, the early modern reform movement made men's masculinity and status as gentlemen contingent on achieving and maintaining dominance without brutality. On the other hand, domestic violence can be seen as one point on a continuum of power and control behaviors. Rather than using a simple hierarchy of tactics that would automatically see the physical as worse than other kinds of threatening behavior, a feminist model looks instead at dominance. This definition calls Petruchio's method abusive because it creates a coercive emotional bond based on fear and intimidation.

Kate and Petruchio Are Rowdy Rebels in Zeffirelli's Film

Jack J. Jorgens

Of the many film adaptations of *The Taming of the Shrew*, Franco Zeffirelli's 1968 production is perhaps the most maligned by critics and the most enjoyed by fans of Richard Burton and Elizabeth Taylor. Jack J. Jorgens, author of *Shakespeare on Film*, describes the film as a "Saturnalian revel." In ancient Rome Saturnalia was the festival in honor of Saturn, god of agriculture. It was celebrated in December with seven days of unrestrained disorder: Presents were exchanged and all people, even slaves, were freed from customary restraints. When Jorgens calls the film a "Saturnalian revel," he alludes to the "exhilaration of holiday" that reverses the order of the everyday world and frees individuals to be wildly unreasonable.

In this excerpt from *Shakespeare on Film*, Jorgens explains that the Zeffirelli film replaces the Christopher Sly frame plot with a new frame: Saturnalian celebration at the beginning of a school term. In the upside-down world of holiday celebration, songs and laughter disrupt seriousness and dignity. In this context, the taming becomes a mutual testing and schooling, and Kate and Petruchio's joint assault on such Paduan values as materialism and hypocrisy becomes central. Kate and Petruchio, who preside over this holiday world as the Lord and Lady of Misrule, exemplify release from imprisoning social expectations. They lead the society toward renewal, yet they are rebels to the end. When the holiday revels end, they maintain their independence by leaving Paduan society, Kate in the lead, Petruchio chasing her.

Franco Zeffirelli, in his boisterous film of *Shrew,* which pits Richard Burton against Elizabeth Taylor, plays up the romance and sentiment, tones down the realism, and revels in the farce. Petruchio and Kate are in love from the moment they set eyes on each other. Their struggle, really a mutual taming, is "the old game"—they test each other, school each other (the other schoolmasters are fakes). When they come to an agreement, it is much more like real-life marriage than the pallid Lucentio-Bianca soap bubble which is pricked in the end. Crass, drunken, self-serving, and materialistic at the beginning, Petruchio, without being rendered impotent, becomes civilized, witty, and dignified by the end. Twice Kate chooses Petruchio over the collection of fops and old men in Padua: by maintaining silence behind the stained glass window when Petruchio announces their wedding on Sunday, and by following him in the rain when he leaves her at Padua's gates and rides toward his crumbling, moth-eaten mansion.

THE "TAMING"

Petruchio's "taming" of Kate in this film has several dimensions. He is the plebeian, taking down a peg a spoiled, egotistical, well-fed, rich girl, teaching her about humility, patience, and recognizing a will other than her own. He is the bohemian teaching her to disdain wealth and luxury, to avoid the bourgeois obsession with appearances and a confusion of values by subjecting her to wetness, cold, fatigue, hunger, pain, and the ridicule of her inferiors. Petruchio, who tests the silver of Baptista's goblets before broaching the subject of marriage and cries "my twenty thousand crowns!" as Kate jumps out the window to escape him, changes too. Like most good teachers, he learns as he teaches.

> To me she's married, not unto my clothes.
> . . . .
> Well, come my Kate; we will unto your father's
> Even in these honest mean habiliments.
> Our purses shall be proud, our garments poor,
> For 'tis the mind that makes the body rich;
> And as the sun breaks through the darkest clouds
> So honor peereth in the meanest habit.

Petruchio is also a playful actor who, unlike the uncreative maskers and unconscious hypocrites of Padua, enjoys taking on roles, is self-aware, and has a sense of irony.

In the beginning, Kate is encased in the role of "shrew," cast in it by frightened, ineffectual men and crafty (though on the surface, submissive) Bianca and kept in it by her refusal to capitulate. She is trapped in a negative image of everything in Padua that she hates, and in that sense she is an imitation of it. Petruchio, her knight in tarnished armor, opposes the frozen, the negative, the uncreative. As D.A. Traversi said, "Petruchio is in effect revealing the *real* Kate to herself. . . ." In cursing him, fighting him, fleeing him, Kate is infinitely more alive and inventive than in dealing with lesser men. Perhaps she learns humility, but she also learns not to be tied to the literal when she must say it is seven o'clock when it is two, or when she must call the sun the moon. In one of the funniest scenes in the film, Kate learns that her husband's "commands" are an invitation to humorous invention. With delicious, devilish innocence, she greets grey-bearded Vincentio as a budding virgin whose parents are blessed in "her." Greeted with his bewildered look as he peers around the head of his horse, she realizes her "mistake" and delivers a mock apology for having her eyes dazzled "by the . . . sun?" (she looks to Petruchio; he nods yes). By raining blows on his servants (the first time we see Petruchio he chases Grumio around the fire, boots him, and rams him into Hortensio's door), making impossible demands, and causing the faults he scolds (he trips the servant who brings the water), by decimating the fashionable clothes prepared for Kate to wear to Bianca's wedding and placing the blame on the poor craftsmen, Petruchio shows Kate her own image. He forces her to see that she must be more forgiving. "Patience," she says, "I pray you, 'twas a fault unwilling." "I pray you, husband, be not so disquiet. The meat was well if you were so contented."

PETRUCHIO: First kiss me Kate, and we will.
KATE: What, in the middle of the street?
PETRUCHIO: What, art thou ashamed of me?
KATE: No sir, God forbid, but ashamed to kiss.
PETRUCHIO: Why then let's home again. Come sirrah, let's away.
KATE: Nay, I will give thee a kiss. Now pray thee, love, stay.

(In the film, Kate holds her own, for she gives him a most unsatisfying peck on the nose.) What he demands, in place of both conformity and rebellion, is tolerance, strong bonds between people, kindness, forgiveness.

THE "SUBMISSION" SPEECH

For Zeffirelli, Kate's "submission" at the end is a kind of *rite de passage,* a demonstration that she understands what

Petruchio has been trying to teach her. After a taste of domestic warfare with Petruchio, a close look at the meanness and vulgarity of the widow and Bianca, and a glance at the children playing with the dogs before the lavish banquet table, Kate seizes the opportunity of the wager to make a pact with Petruchio. With delightful irony, she, who has terrified men by smashing furniture, bellowing, and raining blows on them, bodily hauls the widow and Bianca before their husbands and describes the *frailty* of women. Using her new-found sense of role playing, she uncovers the real shrews and feeds the males present such an eloquent and unconditional surrender to male domination that they are all taken in. But the speech isn't really to them; it is to Petruchio. Beneath her irony, she enunciates the paradox at the heart of love in all of Shakespeare's romantic comedies: give all and you will get all. Kate's fluid shifts in tone, playful hyperbole, love of doing the unexpected, and obvious awareness of her double audience constitute her farewell to the narrowness and rigidities of Kate the shrew. Her offer of "love, fair looks, and true obedience" to Petruchio's "*honest* will," an important qualification, confirms her new-found humility and expresses gratitude for his freeing her from a sterile role. This time there is no hesitation when he asks for a kiss. And if the audience has missed the point and thinks Kate's spirit broken, to the delight of the crowd in the film while Petruchio triumphs over the losers of the wager, Kate sneaks out of the room and makes him begin the chase anew. . . .

THE REBELS

In filming *Shrew*, Zeffirelli obviously provided a pleasant vehicle for Richard Burton and Elizabeth Taylor. But he also redefined, perhaps even revealed, its central action. For most critics and directors, the essence of the play is the "taming" of Kate, or at least the mutual taming of Kate and Petruchio; and certainly the director's radical compression of the Bianca plot makes them even more prominent. But, important as it is, the "taming" is not the heart of the film. Rather, it is the good-natured but thorough assault of Kate and Petruchio on Padua and Paduan values. Zeffirelli turns loose two rebels against hypocrites, greedy pantaloons, time-servers, blind idealists, tricky maidens, and crafty widows. They declare war on respectability, duty, religion, sighing literary romance, and narrowing materialism. . . .

HOLIDAY FRAME STORY

By removing Shakespeare's frame story of Christopher Sly and replacing it with a frame of his own—the saturnalian revels [feasting and unrestrained merrymaking] of the students of Padua—Zeffirelli emphasizes that *Shrew* is also a "festive comedy" saturated with the exhilaration of holiday, that Petruchio and Kate are allied with the saturnalian forces which stand the everyday on its head and turn reason inside out. As Zeffirelli sees it, the comedy is not primarily about a taming, but about a release of Dionysian [recklessly uninhibited—from Dionysus, Greek god of wine, fertility, and drama] energies. As in Alf Sjoberg's *Miss Julie* and Fellini's *Amarcord,* the opening saturnalian ritual defines what follows.

When the film opens, Lucentio and Tranio arrive in Padua on the first day of the new academic year. It is first celebrated solemnly as they witness a beautiful cathedral service in which a boys' choir sings and a Bishop leads the students in prayer. But suddenly a cannon is fired and pandemonium reigns as Zeffirelli provides us with a marvelous condensation of saturnalian motifs. Death, the archenemy of comedy, is mocked as a decorum-shattering funeral winds its way through the streets. A mitred Bishop wearing a mask of a pig strides with great dignity at the head of the procession of mourners carrying a staff crowned with a grinning skull sporting a rakishly slanted turban. In place of the beautiful choir music, we hear raucous songs and obscene chants. The "corpse" (the Old Year) is a skinny, lecherous old man in a white nightcap and nightgown who will not stay dead and has to be forcibly restrained from attacking women (some of them students in drag) along the way. He is treated most indecorously—pummeled with a broom, shaken, tossed high in the air and caught on his bier. The figurative royalty of the procession are the King and Queen, represented by giant masks, but the real queen—the Madonna—is a giant whore who displays her mammoth breasts and strides brassily down the street on foot-high chopines [shoes with thick cork soles]. Chivalry, embodying the height of medieval civilization and encompassing religion, feudal loyalty, and romance, is reduced to a ludicrous knight on a hobby horse, wielding a padded, three-pronged lance. Nearly everyone in the procession wears a mask, many with animalistic features, symbolizing the casting off of civilized identities for more elemental ones. What seems to be an unexpectedly romantic, gentle song sung by several revellers to Bianca, as a figure in a beaked mask lowers a hook to lift her veil, turns out to be bawdy: ". . . give me leave / To do for thee all that Adam did for Eve / I'll do it well, gentle maid, I'll do it well."

This rowdy procession with its chaos of shouts, songs, and shrieks of laughter, completely disrupts the daily routine in Padua, routs seriousness and pretensions to dignity, overturns the hierarchies of power, and dissolves boredom and drudgery. It challenges the populace, tests their sexual prowess, creative energy, thirst, appetites, and late-night endurance. It renews communal feeling by replacing social and economic competition with an orgy of hospitality. Part of the idyll is that modern urban paranoia is banished and creative anarchy reigns, cementing the society together and making life—fraught as it is with failure, sickness, and death—more tolerable.

THE LORD AND LADY OF MISRULE

This new frame was a perceptive stroke, and it is interesting to see how many of its themes carry over into the other parts of both play and film—the theme of masking, for instance, of confused or transformed identities. Everyone in the play wears a mask of some sort: Lucentio and Hortensio the masks of "schoolmasters," Kate is "the shrew," Petruchio "the patient wooer," Tranio is "Lucentio," and Bianca "the meek and dutiful daughter." Vincentio has the dreamlike experience of meeting his own double. The overturning of hierarchies also recurs: daughters and sons rule the fathers, servants become masters. In both the opening procession and the rest of the film the central activity is male pursuit of the female. Kate refers specifically to the Madonna-whore when she shrieks at her father "would you make a whore of me among these mates?" Above all, it becomes clear that in assaulting conventional society, Petruchio and Kate are Lord and Lady of Misrule, two bulls crashing through the Paduan china shop. Their courtship burlesques courtly love. Petruchio, who has absorbed Christopher Sly's coarseness and love for the bottle, is no genteel poetical wooer, and Kate, who hurls stools and kegs at suitors and breaks lutes over their heads, lacks the disposition of a Maiden Fair. Their destruction, like that in the Marx brothers' *Night at the Opera*, is an expression of contempt both for culture and for things (recall Petruchio's schoolings), an assault on the old order.

The life of decorative luxury, condensed by Zeffirelli into the wine glasses, rich curtains, stuffed bed, and bath water strewn with rose petals at Hortensio's house, is put in its place by Petruchio's bumblings and smashings, socks with holes, and delicate swishing aside of the rose petals to dampen his fingers so as to daub his eyes and ears.

The wedding of Kate and Petruchio is, like the funeral procession, a travesty and a sacrilege. Petruchio arrives two-and-a-half hours late, drunk, dressed in garish clothes (traditional for the Lord of Misrule) including a huge striped pillow adorned with pheasant feathers, carrying dead game birds, and blowing kisses to ladies in the crowd. Enraged, Kate invites him with a smile, then shoves him down the steps, puts down her veil, and races down the aisle, with Petruchio, the children, and guests scrambling in behind her. And all the while, an incongruously beautiful, slow "Gloria" is sounded by organ and chorus in the background, recalling the opening religious ceremony. Once at the altar, Petruchio falls asleep, has a coughing fit, gulps down the holy wine with an oath, shoves the mousy, protesting priest to the floor, fumbles for the ring and laughing stupidly displays it to the crowd. He caps his performance by stopping Kate's mouth with a kiss at the "will" of "*I will not!*" The traditional wedding dinner is deflated in midjollity as Petruchio carries Kate out into the rain and leaves the guests to celebrate without them. It is replaced by the inelegant, parodic repast of half-plucked chickens and pudding poured over someone's hat, served by filthy, leering cutthroats amid the wreckage at Petruchio's house; and even this is delayed by Petruchio's comically prolonged grace and then destroyed as he rages that the meal is not fit for the starving bride. The wedding night becomes a blow on the head with a warming pan, a bed ripped apart, and—for the groom—a night on a hard bench.

Also following Shakespeare's lead, Zeffirelli turns the wooing of Kate into a mock epic, continuing the travesty of chivalric valor in the opening procession. When Petruchio, Hortensio, Gremio, and the rest back away in fear upon hearing Bianca scream, our hero boldly declares:

> Think you a little din can daunt mine ears?
> Have I not in my time heard lions roar?
> Have I not heard the sea, puffed up with winds,
> Rage like an angry boar chafed with sweat?
> Have I not heard great ordnance in the field
> And heaven's artillery thunder in the skies?

Have I not in a pitched battle heard
Loud 'larums, neighing steeds, and trumpets' clang?
And do you tell me of a woman's tongue?

Then a spirited Sousa-like match is played by a totally anach-
ronistic full marching band on the sound track as Petruchio
strides down the street, followed by lesser mortals, to ring the
bell at Baptista's house. In another display of comic heroism,
Petruchio, while casting the commercial values of Padua in the
teeth of the guests ("she is my goods, my chattels") "rescues"
Kate from the bridal dinner (like Erroll Flynn) to the accom-
paniment of shouts, thunder, and lightning flashing against
Grumio's pathetically short sword (Petruchio has lost his).

SOCIAL ORDER RESTORED

In "comedies of the green world," as Northrop Frye calls
them, it is usual at the end for "a new society to crystallize
around the hero." The Lord and Lady of Misrule do not reject
order altogether. They simply seek a period of release from
imprisoning things and rigid identities in order to humanize
society and make discoveries about themselves. Like the
lovers and Dukes who flee to the forest in *A Midsummer
Night's Dream* and in *As You Like It*, or Bassanio who voyages
to Belmont to hazard for Portia, Petruchio and Kate journey
from the city to their decrepit country house, where they are
reborn. But once Kate has invaded the male enclave and restored it to order, and the seeds of harmony between herself
and Petruchio are sown, like the other voyagers, they make a
return. The concluding banquet celebrates a new harmony
between parents and children, the old order and the new.

Still, in the film the reconciliation and transformation at
the end are not complete. At the dinner Bianca's mask drops,
now that she is a wife, and, as was foreshadowed in her earlier outbursts of temper, she becomes a "shrew." The joke is
on the newly married men, for not only have they lost the
bet, they have yet to fight the battles that Kate and Petruchio
have fought, and, quite frankly, they don't look up to it. As in
Shakespeare, the hero and heroine do not remain at the center of the supposedly renewed society but assert their superiority by leaving it. Petruchio is ultimately bored with
Padua ("eat and drink, eat and drink") and finds chasing the
playful, inviting Kate much more interesting. For once the
rebels in a comedy are not absorbed by society, but maintain
their independence to the last.

CHRONOLOGY

1509

Italian writer Ariosto's *I Suppositi*, containing a story similar to the subplot of *The Taming of the Shrew*, appears.

1543

Polish astronomer Nicolaus Copernicus introduces the idea of a sun- rather than earth-centered universe in his *On the Revolutions*.

1550

A ballad, "A Merry Jest of a Shrewd and Curst Wife Lapped in Morel's Skin," sometimes listed as a source for *The Taming of the Shrew*, is printed.

1557

William Shakespeare's parents, John Shakespeare and Mary Arden, are married.

1558

Elizabeth I becomes queen of England, initiating the Elizabethan age.

1561

Philosopher and statesman Francis Bacon is born.

1564

William Shakespeare is born in the village of Stratford in central England; his noted contemporary, writer Christopher Marlowe, is also born.

1566

Ovid's *Metamorphoses* are translated by Arthur Golding; George Gascoigne's play, *Supposes*, a translation of Ariosto's *I Suppositi*, is first performed.

1572

Playwright Ben Jonson, who will later become a rival of Shakespeare's, is born.

1573

Gascoigne's *Supposes*, the source for the subplot of *The Taming of the Shrew*, is published.

1576

London's first public theater, the Theatre, opens.

1577

Raphael Holinshed's *Chronicles*, a primary source for many of Shakespeare's plays, appears.

1577–1580

Englishman Sir Francis Drake sails around the world.

1582

William Shakespeare marries Anne Hathaway.

1583

Shakespeare's daughter Susanna is born.

1585

Shakespeare's twins, Hamnet and Judith, are born.

CA. 1587

Shakespeare leaves Stratford and heads for London to pursue a career in the theater; *Supposes* is republished.

1588

England wins a major victory over Spain by defeating the mighty Spanish Armada.

1589

The earliest probable date for *The Taming of the Shrew*.

CA. 1590–1593

Shakespeare writes *The Comedy of Errors*; *Henry VI, parts 1, 2, and 3*; and *Richard III*.

1592

Robert Greene refers to Shakespeare as an "upstart crow" in his pamphlet *Greene's Groatsworth of Wit*.

1593–1594

The usual date given for *The Taming of the Shrew*.

1594

"A Pleasant Conceited Historie called the taming of a Shrew" is printed; it is now considered a "bad quarto" of Shakespeare's play.

CA. 1594–1600

Shakespeare writes *Much Ado About Nothing; As You Like It; Twelfth Night; Richard II; Henry IV, parts 1 and 2; Henry V;* and *Julius Caesar.*

1597

Shakespeare buys New Place, the largest home in Stratford.

1598–1599

The Globe Theater opens; Shakespeare owns one-eighth of its profits.

1600

In Italy, the church burns priest Giordano Bruno at the stake for advocating the idea that the stars are distant suns, each having its own planets.

CA. 1600–1607

Shakespeare writes what will later be acknowledged as his greatest tragedies: *Hamlet, Othello, King Lear, Macbeth,* and *Antony and Cleopatra.*

1601

John Shakespeare dies.

1603

Queen Elizabeth dies; James I becomes king of England; England conquers Ireland.

1607

English settlers establish the colony of Jamestown, giving England a permanent foothold in North America.

1608–1613

Shakespeare writes *Coriolanus, The Winter's Tale, The Tempest, Henry VIII,* and *The Two Noble Kinsmen.*

1610

Italian scholar Galileo Galilei points his newly built telescope at the planet Jupiter and discovers four orbiting moons, proving conclusively that all heavenly bodies do not revolve around Earth.

1611

The King James Version of the Bible is published; John Fletcher's sequel to *The Taming of the Shrew*, called *The Tamer Tamed*, is written.

1616

Shakespeare dies.

1623

Anne Hathaway Shakespeare dies; the First Folio, a complete collection of Shakespeare's works, is published; *The Taming of the Shrew* appears in print for the first time in the First Folio.

1633

The Taming of the Shrew is performed for King Charles I.

1663

The last recorded performance of *The Taming of the Shrew* until the middle of the nineteenth century.

1667

John Lacey's adaptation, *Sauny the Scot: Or, The Taming of the Shrew: A Comedy*, is performed.

1735

James Worsdale's adaptation, *A Cure for a Scold*, is published.

1754

David Garrick's adaptation, *Catherine and Petruchio*, is performed and continues to be staged for one hundred years.

1844

Benjamin Webster revives Shakespeare's *The Taming of the Shrew*.

1887

The first American performance of Shakespeare's *The Taming of the Shrew* is in Augustin Daly's Theatre, New York.

1948

Cole Porter's musical *Kiss Me Kate* is produced.

1960

John Barton's Royal Shakespeare Company production of *The Taming of the Shrew* uses the entire Christopher Sly framework from the anonymous "A Shrew."

1966

Franco Zeffirelli's film *Taming of the Shrew* stars Richard Burton and Elizabeth Taylor.

1975

Charles Marowitz's adaptation, *The Shrew*, creates a brutalized, brainwashed Kate.

1978

Michael Bogdanov's Royal Shakespeare Company production focuses on the contemporary relevance of class oppression and female exploitation in *The Taming of the Shrew.*

1980

Jonathan Miller's BBC/Time-Life version presents *The Taming of the Shrew* from an Elizabethan Puritan's view.

1986

Popular television show, *Moonlighting*, presents an adaptation called "Petruchio and Kate."

FOR FURTHER RESEARCH

TEXT AND CRITICISM OF *THE TAMING OF THE SHREW*

Sylvan Barnet, "Shakespeare: An Overview," *The Taming of the Shrew*. New York: Signet, 1986.

John C. Bean, "Comic Structure and the Humanizing of Kate in *The Taming of the Shrew*," in *The Woman's Part: Feminist Criticism of Shakespeare*. Ed. Carolyn Ruth Swift Lenz, Gayle Greene, and Carol Thomas Neely. Urbana: University of Illinois Press, 1980.

David Bevington, ed., *The Complete Works of Shakespeare*. 4th ed. New York: HarperCollins, 1992.

——, *The Taming of the Shrew*. New York: Bantam, 1988.

——, *William Shakespeare: Four Comedies*. New York: Bantam, 1988.

Robert G. Blake, "Critical Evaluation" in *A Reader's Guide to Shakespeare* by Joseph Rosenblum. New York: Barnes & Noble Books, 1999.

Lynda E. Boose, "*The Taming of the Shrew*, Good Husbandry, and Enclosure," in *Shakespeare Reread*. Ed. Russ McDonald. Ithaca, NY: Cornell University Press, 1994.

Charles Boyce, *Shakespeare A to Z: The Essential Reference to His Plays, His Poems, His Life and Times, and More*. New York: Facts On File, 1990.

Jan Harold Brunvand, The Taming of the Shrew: *A Comparative Study of Oral and Literary Versions*. Unpublished Ph.D. dissertation. Indiana University, 1961.

Emily Detmer, "Civilizing Subordination: Domestic Violence and *The Taming of the Shrew*." *Shakespeare Quarterly*, Fall 1997, pp. 273–94.

Frances E. Dolan, ed., The Taming of the Shrew: *Texts and Contexts*. New York: Bedford Books of St. Martin's Press, 1996.

Juliet Dusinberre, "*The Taming of the Shrew*: Women, Acting, and Power," *Studies in the Literary Imagination*, Spring 1993, pp. 67–84.

Norrie Epstein, *The Friendly Shakespeare: A Thoroughly Painless Guide to the Best of the Bard.* New York: Viking Penguin, 1993.

Harold C. Goddard, *The Meaning of Shakespeare.* Chicago: University of Chicago Press, 1951.

Robert B. Heilman, "The *Taming* Untamed, Or, The Return of the Shrew," *Modern Language Quarterly* #27, June 1966, pp. 147–61.

Graham Holderness, ed., *The Shakespeare Myth.* Manchester: Manchester University Press, 1988.

———, *The Taming of the Shrew.* Shakespeare in Performance. New York and Manchester: Manchester University Press, 1989.

J. Dennis Huston, "'To Make a Puppet': Play and Play-Making in *The Taming of the Shrew*," *Shakespeare Studies*, 1976, pp. 73–88.

Ben Jonson, "To the Memory of My Beloved, the Author Mr. William Shakespeare," Prefixed to the Shakespeare First Folio of 1623.

Jack J. Jorgens, "Franco Zeffirelli's *Taming of the Shrew.*" *Shakespeare on Film.* Lanham, MD: University Press of America, 1991.

Coppelia Kahn, "*The Taming of the Shrew*: Shakespeare's Mirror of Marriage," *Modern Language Studies* #5, Spring 1975, pp. 88–102.

Alvin B. Kernan, *The Playwright as Magician.* New Haven, CT: Yale University Press, 1979.

Francois Laroque, *The Age of Shakespeare.* New York: Harry N. Abrams, 1993.

Harry Levin, Introduction to *The Riverside Shakespeare.* 2nd. ed. Boston: Houghton Mifflin, 1997.

Gareth Lloyd Evans, *The Upstart Crow.* Ed. and rev. Barbara Lloyd Evans. London: J.M. Dent & Sons, 1982.

Russ McDonald, ed., *The Bedford Companion to Shakespeare.* New York: Bedford Books of St. Martin's Press, 1996.

Brian Morris, ed., *The Arden Edition of the Works of William Shakespeare:* The Taming of the Shrew. London: Methuen, 1981.

Leah Scragg, *Shakespeare's Mouldy Tales: Recurrent Plot Motifs in Shakespearean Drama.* London: Longman Group UK, 1992.

Michael West, "The Folk Background of Petruchio's Wooing Dance: Male Supremacy in *The Taming of the Shrew,*" *Shakespeare Studies,* 1974, pp. 65–73.

SHAKESPEARE'S LIFE AND TIMES

Gerald E. Bentley, *Shakespeare: A Biographical Handbook.* Westport, CT: Greenwood, 1986.

Roland M. Frye, *Shakespeare's Life and Times: A Pictorial Record.* Princeton, NJ: Princeton University Press, 1967.

Francois Laroque, *The Age of Shakespeare.* New York: Harry N. Abrams, 1993

———, *Shakespeare's Festive World: Elizabethan Seasonal Entertainment and the Professional Stage.* Cambridge: Cambridge University Press, 1991.

Peter Levi, *The Life and Times of William Shakespeare.* New York: Henry Holt, 1989.

Peter Quennell, *Shakespeare: A Biography.* Cleveland: World, 1963.

A.L. Rowse, *Shakespeare the Man.* New York: Harper and Row, 1973.

———, *William Shakespeare: A Biography.* New York: Harper and Row, 1963.

SHAKESPEAREAN THEATER AND FILM

John C. Adams, *The Globe Playhouse: Its Design and Equipment.* 2nd ed. Cambridge, MA: Harvard University Press, 1942. Reprinted Barnes and Noble, 1961.

Sally Beauman, *The Royal Shakespeare Company: A History of Ten Decades.* Oxford: Oxford University Press, 1982.

John R. Brown, *William Shakespeare: Writing for Performance.* New York: St. Martin's Press, 1996.

John Collick, *Shakespeare, Cinema, and Society.* New York and Manchester: Manchester University Press, 1989.

Cecile DeBanke, *Shakespearean Stage Production, Then and Now.* London: Hutchinson, 1954.

Peter Donaldson, *Shakespearean Films/Shakespearean Directors.* Boston: Unwin Hyman, 1990.

Charles W. Eckert, *Focus on Shakespearean Film.* Englewood Cliffs, NJ: Prentice-Hall, 1972.

John Elsom, *Post-War British Theater Criticism.* London: Routledge and Kegan Paul, 1981.

Andrew Gurr, *Playgoing in Shakespeare's London.* Cambridge: Cambridge University Press, 1987.

G.B. Harrison, *Elizabethan Plays and Players.* Ann Arbor: University of Michigan Press, 1956.

Jack J. Jorgens, *Shakespeare on Film.* Bloomington: Indiana University Press, 1977.

Roger Manvell, *Shakespeare and the Film.* London: Praeger, 1971.

Robert Speaight, *Shakespeare on the Stage.* London: Collins, 1973.

Arthur C. Sprague, *Shakespeare and the Actor's Stage Business in His Plays (1660–1905).* Cambridge, MA: Harvard University Press, 1944.

GENERAL GUIDES TO SHAKESPEARE'S PLAYS

Isaac Asimov, *Asimov's Guide to Shakespeare.* New York: Avenel Books, 1978.

Charles Boyce, *Shakespeare: A to Z: The Essential Reference to His Plays, His Poems, His Life and Times, and More.* New York: Facts On File, 1990.

Norrie Epstein, *The Friendly Shakespeare: A Thoroughly Painless Guide to the Best of the Bard.* New York: Viking Penguin, 1993.

G. Blakemore Evans, gen. ed., *The Riverside Shakespeare.* 2nd ed. Boston: Houghton Mifflin, 1997.

Harley Granville-Barker and G.B. Harrison, eds., *A Companion to Shakespeare Studies.* Cambridge: Cambridge University Press, 1959.

Karl J. Holzknecht, *The Backgrounds of Shakespeare's Plays.* New York: American, 1950.

Kenneth Muir and Samuel Schoenbaum, eds., *A New Companion to Shakespeare Studies.* Oxford: Oxford University Press, 1971.

GENERAL SHAKESPEAREAN ANALYSIS AND CRITICISM

C.L. Barber, *Shakespeare's Festive Comedy.* Princeton, NJ: Princeton University Press, 1972.

Ralph Berry, *Shakespeare's Comedies.* Princeton, NJ: Princeton University Press, 1972.

Andrew C. Bradley, *Shakespearean Tragedy.* New York: Viking Penguin, 1991.

Lily B. Campbell, *Shakespeare's Tragic Heroes: Slaves of Passion.* 1930. Reprint, New York: Barnes and Noble, 1968.

Edmund K. Chambers, *William Shakespeare: A Study of Facts and Problems.* New York: Oxford University Press, 1989.

William Empson, *Essays on Shakespeare.* Cambridge: Cambridge University Press, 1986.

M.D. Faber, *The Design Within: Psychoanalytic Approaches to Shakespeare.* New York: Science House, 1970.

Brian Gibbons, *Shakespeare and Multiplicity.* Cambridge: Cambridge University Press, 1993.

Clifford Leech, ed., *Shakespeare: The Tragedies: A Collection of Critical Essays.* Chicago: University of Chicago Press, 1965.

Carolyn R.S. Lenz et al., eds., *The Woman's Part: Feminist Criticism of Shakespeare.* Urbana: University of Illinois Press, 1980.

Maynard Mack Jr., *Killing the King: Three Studies in Shakespeare's Tragic Structure.* New Haven, CT: Yale University Press, 1973.

Robert Ornstein, *Shakespeare's Comedies from Roman Farce to Romantic Mystery.* Newark: University of Delaware Press, 1986.

Clarice Swisher, ed., *Readings on the Tragedies of William Shakespeare.* San Diego: Greenhaven Press, 1996.

Works by William Shakespeare

Editor's Note: Many of the dates on this list are approximate. Because manuscripts identified with the date of writing do not exist, scholars have determined the most accurate available date, either of the writing or of the first production of each play.

1 Henry VI (1591)

2 and *3 Henry VI* (1591–1592)

Richard III; The Comedy of Errors (1592–1593)

Sonnets (1592–1600)

Titus Andronicus; The Taming of the Shrew; The Two Gentlemen of Verona; Love's Labour's Lost; publication of *Venus and Adonis* (1593)

Publication of *The Rape of Lucrece* (1594)

A Midsummer Night's Dream; Romeo and Juliet; Richard II (1594–1595)

The Merchant of Venice (1595–1596)

King John (1596)

1 Henry IV (1597)

2 Henry IV; Much Ado About Nothing (1598)

Henry V; As You Like It; Julius Caesar; The Merry Wives of Windsor; publication of "The Passionate Pilgrim" (1599)

Twelfth Night; Hamlet; Troilus and Cressida (1600–1601)

"The Phoenix and the Turtle" (1601)

All's Well That Ends Well (1603)

Othello; Measure for Measure (1604)

King Lear (1605)

Macbeth (1606)

Antony and Cleopatra; Coriolanus; Timon of Athens; Pericles (1607–1609)

Sonnets and "A Lover's Complaint" first published by Thomas Thorpe (1609)

Cymbeline (1610)

The Winter's Tale (1610–1611)

The Tempest (1611)

Henry VIII [possibly a collaboration] (1612–1613)

The Two Noble Kinsmen [in collaboration with John Fletcher] (1613)

INDEX